# Rituals FOR Transformation

## 108 DAY JOURNEY TO YOUR SACRED LIFE

Briana and Dr. Peter Borten

Printed in the United States of America

Second Edition, 2019
ISBN 978-1-7337369-0-9

The Dragontree
Portland, Oregon

www.thedragontree.com

# WELCOME

Thank you, dear friend, for taking this step.

You're about to begin a journey that will change you. If you're someone who fears change, rest assured that the change we're talking about is for your *highest good*. This means it may not be what's easiest or fastest, but it's the deepest and the *realest* kind of change. This also means it's not going to demand that you give up anything of *true value*.

Waking up and opening yourself to true happiness won't make you leave your spouse, children, friends, religion, or job. Nor will it require you to give up beer, or wearing nice clothes, or having an expensive car, if you enjoy those things. But if your happiness has been *dependent* on the state of your relationships, finances, health, or possessions, this will be a new way of living. As you get better at accessing happiness and peace in any circumstance, you may choose to let go of elements of your life that aren't healthy for you, but you'll be able to do so with clarity and kindness.

How would it be if you felt *trust* rather than *fear* in times of uncertainty?

What if you were at *peace* with your body, regardless of its appearance or function?

How would life be different if you weren't controlled by your thoughts and emotions?

What would life be like if you were able to focus on all the things you're grateful for, rather than being consumed by the problems?

How would it feel to be okay with whatever happens?

What would it be like to experience yourself as one with the Source of everything, playing in this life while always remembering that you are loved and connected?

Sound good? We're with you. This is the kind of life we want, too. We're engaged in this work day in and day out, and we'll be doing it for the rest of our lives. There's a challenge and an opportunity in every moment. And there's great joy and inspiration in sharing this process with others. That's why we decided to write this book – so there will be more of us consciously walking the path together, sharing support, shining a light on darkness and untruth, jointly rising to the occasion.

Our earlier work focused more on tangible interventions people could make for better lives – things like dietary modification, community building, and goal setting. We were directing our efforts toward the kinds of changes most people want, in a way that made sense to them. We offered multi-dimensional approaches to achieving measurable outcomes – more money, a better job, a new relationship, a healthier body.

While we stand by the value of these teachings and have witnessed many dramatic transformations, we also saw that we weren't getting to the real root of many people's problems. The most revolutionary transformations occurred not when a person's circumstances changed, but when they experienced a fundamental change of perspective. Meanwhile, numerous members of the community that has formed around our healthcare practices, spas, books, and courses have expressed an interest in going deeper.

That's why we're aiming for a different place with this book – we're going right for the heart of your beliefs. This book is a structure through which to safely challenge your limitations and explore new possibilities. You'll play in this structure for 108 days – the length of time we feel is most likely to produce lasting change. And if you do that, you'll inevitably grow through this process and experience more love, peace, happiness, and freedom. We promise.

# WHY US?

We've undertaken diverse explorations of spirituality and philosophy. We've learned from great teachers. We have degrees in Eastern medicine and years of experience working with clients. And we have wonderful, abundant, joyous lives. If that helps your mind feel better, great. But these "qualifications" alone don't make us worthy teachers.

In fact, you should probably be skeptical of anyone professing to have lessons that the whole world needs. So, we'd like to assure you that we're not gurus, experts, or masters. To take on such a title would imply that we know all there is to know, or that we've achieved all there is to achieve. Such arrogance would close the doors to our learning and we want no such thing. We intend to be students forever, and we humble ourselves to the Great Teacher that the Universe is.

We want to walk this path alongside you, not ahead of you.

We're not the Source of anything we present here. We've come up with what we hope will be accurate words, useful metaphors, and an effective presentation, but we're simply doing our best to *pass on* the perennial wisdom that has been imparted to us.

Instead of mastery what we have is devotion. We are devoted to humanity, to healing, to evolving, to awakening, to service, and we're devoted to Love. We've been doing this for a while, we're committed, and it's had a tremendous impact on our lives. We've found that the more we open ourselves to the guidance of the universe, the more clearly we hear and see new ways to help others and ourselves. Central to what we've learned is that we and you are deeply connected. Thus, our commitment to ourselves is a commitment to you. We came to a point at which we saw that we could go no further in our own healing without helping the world to do the same.

We try to be good listeners and to hear what speaks to our hearts. We add all of it to our ever-evolving understanding of life and the vocabulary we utilize to point our clients and readers toward greater freedom and peace. This is us being real with you. What you *can* trust is our intentions.

~

We wouldn't be able to bring you this book without the tremendous minds and spirits of those who came before us. Some of these influences include: Lao Zi, Carl Jung, G. I. Gurdjieff, Zhuangzi, Confucius, Alan Watts, Rumi, Nisargadatta Maharaj, Henry David Thoreau, Meister Eckhart, Robert Svoboda and Aghori Vimalananda, Adyashanti, Byron Katie, Yogi Bhajan, Thich Nhat Hanh, Jon Kabat-Zinn, Ram Dass, Helen Schucman, Sirinam Khalsa, Gurunam Khalsa, Amma Sri Karunamayi, Abraham, Ken Wilber, Don Miguel Ruiz, Hale Dwoskin, Emmanuel, Gregory Fong, Christoper Wallis, Eckhart Tolle, Dan Millman, Vadim Zeland, Carlos Castaneda, Mike Dooley, Jean Klein, Acharya Buddharakkhita, Matt Garrigan, and many more. We encourage you to check out their work.

# HOW TO DO THIS & WHAT TO EXPECT

**Plan and Set an Intention**

Look ahead at your schedule and plan your start date. You don't need to have 108 days set aside with absolutely no work, travel, or drama. But if you know you have an upcoming period when it would be difficult to maintain any sort of consistent routine, you may wish to delay your start until after that time. Unforeseen demands are to be expected, though, and continuing with the process has the potential to support you to navigate these demands. In fact, having life challenges while working through the book will provide great opportunities to practice what you're learning.

If you find you simply can't continue with your lessons at some point, mark your place and set the book aside while you manage your life. When you're able to return to it, you can decide whether to pick up where you left off, or to go back a few lessons, or to start the whole thing over.

When you're ready to start, we recommend performing a simple ritual to set the stage for your transformation. At the least, you could take a minute or so to sit in silence and focus on what you want to get out of this process. To take it a little further, you could envision yourself at the end of the 108 days, happier, clearer, more peaceful, or changed in some other way. As you do so, really feel and attempt to experience what that would be like. You might also wish to light a candle, say a prayer, write down an intention, or add other elements to your ritual that will make it feel more significant to you. Fully expect to have a transformation beyond what your mind might consider reasonable. Imagine you're making space in your self-image for this new You to emerge.

**The Lessons**

Each day you'll be presented with a one- or two-sentence lesson and a few paragraphs of explanatory text. The lessons are designed to help you release limiting beliefs, change detrimental habits, open to new ideas, love and forgive yourself and others, access a higher consciousness, and know yourself better. They're laid out in a specific order so that you'll move through multiple thematic arcs nested within each other, in a way that will facilitate healing and awakening at a pace that you can integrate.

Readers familiar with A Course in Miracles (ACIM) will notice some parallels between that text and this one. In particular, ACIM includes a year-long workbook that offers a lesson and meditation for each day, which was deeply inspiring to us. A number of its central teachings — on grievances and forgiveness – also figure significantly into our spiritual worldview. But in the long nights of discussion that led to the decision to write this book, we came to recognize that we have different aims and a different orientation than ACIM – and all the other primary sources we drew from as well.

ACIM has a Christian orientation and male-centric language. Other of our influences are female-centric, or Hindu, or Buddhist, or Nature-oriented. Many sources use special terminology or involve faith in a system of belief that presents a big hurdle for many who are uninitiated. Some texts speak to improving one's psychology and circumstances, and are best for people who want a more happy and comfortable existence. Others speak to awakening entirely from one's identification as a human – to becoming enlightened – and transcending human goals and personal development entirely.

Through hours of dialogue about who our audience is, what this book's goals are, how to be most effective at initiating change in the greatest number of people, and what we would and wouldn't compromise on, the orientation emerged that's presented here. We mean to speak to those who are somewhere between wanting to shape their material lives and awakening to an understanding of reality that puts them at peace with whatever their material circumstances might be. We aimed to avoid explicit religious terminology, a gendered view of Spirit, or to limit access to only those at a certain place in their development. We felt the most responsible approach was to speak to you at numerous levels. These lessons will land in different places within you at different times, likely reaching multiple facets of you simultaneously.

Speaking of terminology, throughout the book we use many different words for what most people call God. We do this for two reasons. The first is to lessen the potential to turn off a reader who has difficulty with any particular term. The second is to remind you that these are all names for the same thing, which is, of course, beyond any name. Any time you encounter one of these words, feel free to substitute another word that works better for you, such as: Spirit, Goddess, Nature, Divine Light, Awareness, Dao, Universe, Holy Spirit, Consciousness, Love, Highest Self, Supreme Oneness, Inner Being, Divine Mother/Father, Jesus, Mohammed, Krishna, Buddha, Lord, etc.

You're going to encounter similar ideas repeatedly. We do this because, if you're like us, you'll need to be exposed to them multiple times before they really sink in. Also, your response to a concept the first time you're exposed to it will be different than when you're re-exposed to it in the new context provided by the lessons you've moved through since then.

Much time, energy, and intention was given to expressing these lessons in language that would be clear, accurate, and effective at promoting change. Whenever trying to convey such deep teachings as these, we're acutely aware of the limitation of words to express something that can really only be experienced. As it says in the first line of the 2000-year-old Daoist classic, *Dao De Ching (The Book of the Virtue of the Way)*, "The Dao that can be spoken of is not the true Dao," meaning, as soon as we attempt to reduce God (Dao) to words, we're bound to fall short.

But, as the Dao De Ching is itself a book, there's a recognition that we're making a compromise. After all, books have *changed our lives*. So, despite the shortcomings of language, it's nonetheless worthwhile to use words to point us in the right direction, toward a *personal experience* of the Truth they're hinting at.

There is truth in so many traditions. All the traditions we mentioned earlier point roughly in the same direction. But in speaking to the part of you that knows this Truth, we chose to be realistic about the fact that, for most people, certain word choices are easier to digest than others, certain philosophies are less dogmatic than others, and certain expressions are more easily disentangled from centuries of human neurosis than others. So, we made many discretionary choices.

We decided these lessons would sink in the best if we wrote them in "second person" – i.e., it's all about *you*. As such, we had to make some assumptions about you. We assumed that you're like us and like most people. We assumed that you are reading this with an open mind. We assumed that you have a sense of humor. It's possible that we assumed wrong and that you may experience some passages as feeling critical or accusatory. We assure you, we feel no hostility toward you and it wasn't our intention to trigger feelings of blame or shame. But we didn't want to sacrifice the effectiveness of the lessons by making the language less pointed. We make pointed observations and ask pointed questions because pointy things get to the point.

Sometimes we opted for wording we felt would be understood by the greatest number of readers, even if it involved slightly imperfect metaphors. Other times, it was vital to be precise, even if the words would be challenging for some. We knew it wasn't possible that all of our choices would be just right for every reader, and that some feathers would get ruffled. We also guessed that some people would be turned off to some or all of the book as a result.

If this is the case for you, try not to throw the baby out with the bathwater. What we're really asking you – what we hope you'll ask *yourself* — is for a *commitment*. By this, we mean an agreement to engage with this material with a spirit of enthusiastic participation. There is something of value here for virtually everyone. If you have a hard time with some of our words or concepts, try to see beyond them to the message that's meant for you. If you give yourself 108 days to heal, discover, and awaken, you *will* benefit from this.

Remember, you bought this book because you wanted something that you hoped the book would help you attain. The only way you'll find out what's possible is by showing up fully. We know how personal one's spiritual beliefs and sensibilities can be. Our intention is always to *expand* your perspective, never to *restrict* it. Our vision of reality may not match 100% with yours, but in everything we present, we do it with an openness. We prefer to err on the side of offering *more freedom* rather than less.

If the language and ideas simply don't work for you, we strongly encourage you to stick with the 108 days you set aside for *you* — even if you decide to throw the book away. But we also urge you to look deeper at the parts that rubbed you the wrong way. If you're willing to hang in there, we ask that you answer these questions honestly for yourself:

1.    Is there an opportunity to learn, heal, or grow from this?
      (If yes, please do so.)

2.    Is there a way you can change the wording that will result in a message that is more in line with your own sensibilities, while still feeling meaningful and uplifting?
      (If yes, please do so.)

3.    Are you willing to be open and continue on with the book, trusting that you will benefit from this process?
      (If yes, please do so.)

It's best to read the lesson for the day *first thing in the morning*. This way it will set a tone for your whole day, and it will allow you to apply the day's lesson to anything and everything that occurs. It also becomes a declaration of your priorities, like saying, "YOU, my Highest Self, are the *most important thing*. More important than email, texts, Facebook, news, or even breakfast." What you get out of these 108 days is directly related to your level of participation.

## Meditate

After you read the lesson, take a few minutes to meditate. You'll notice that we offer some guidance on meditations in the first handful of lessons, but stop reminding you after the first week. A minimum of fifteen minutes of meditation would be ideal, but even *one* minute is better than nothing. A single minute, given your total presence, could change your whole day – and beyond.

There are many ways to meditate, and if you have a method that works for you, you're welcome to stick with that. Otherwise, here's our recommendation.

The vast majority of your waking life is spent in a state of *manipulated awareness* – a state in which your awareness is focused almost entirely on your mind, emotions, and body, all of which are deeply conditioned by your upbringing and environment. Spiritual traditions and modern neurology assert that your consciousness isn't limited to the perception of your own mind and body. Opening your awareness beyond your personal chattering — which is just a small portion of what you are — allows you to access a limitless reservoir of peace, love, and wisdom that's always present. Moreover, it gives you a glimpse of what you *really* are and offers perspective to the life issues that tend to dominate your attention.

So, our main instruction is to do your best in meditation to open yourself to something beyond your mind and emotions, and even beyond your body, without trying to manipulate your experience. This is done by inviting a spaciousness in your awareness and abstaining from filling it with your *stuff*. Instead, just *be* in that space.

It's a good idea to find a comfortable place to sit with closed eyes where you won't be distracted, so that there will be minimal sensory input – either from outside you or from your own uncomfortable body. Ideally, you'll meditate in the same place and time each day. People tend to do well with consistency. Your Being will learn what to do.

If you like, you can make your meditation space special. Some people find it enhances their meditative experience to have a spot designated just for this practice, perhaps with scents, elements, or objects that help you relax and tune in.

To begin your meditation, close your eyes, take one or more deep breaths, and intend to set aside whatever is on your mind or happening in your body. Then imagine you're opening your consciousness deep within yourself and far "outside" yourself. Allow your awareness to go beyond your own thoughts and feelings. And just *rest* in this space without attaching to any of the thoughts or feelings that will inevitably arise. When you notice that you have been focusing on some thought or feeling, just let it go and open your awareness again.

We don't want your meditation practice to just be a closed-eye thinking session, but we do want you to make use of this practice to facilitate insight and healing. So, at the beginning of your meditation, when you first feel this *opening* in your awareness, take the lesson for the day (e.g., "I forgive my body") and place it into this space. You might silently speak it into the space or envision the words dropping into the space, intending that they be heard and received in the farthest reaches of your being – the deepest places within you and the most distant regions imaginable.

Then let it go. Try to refrain from analyzing the words, finding a meaning, or otherwise *figuring things out.* Just let your mind take a break. Meanwhile, gently listen, with your whole awareness, for whatever comes to you (perhaps nothing). If your mind is relentless at monopolizing your attention, try watching your breath – notice how it rises and falls. Don't be attached to having a special experience.

## Set an Intention

In the Intention space, write an intention for the day. Read the lesson and explanation, feel into it in your meditation, and then *make a choice:* What do you intend for today? Generally, this will be a statement that's closely related to the day's lesson. Sometimes you may simply write the lesson word-for-word here. For instance, on the day that you encounter, *I choose my Highest Self,* you might write as your intention, "I chose my Highest Self today," or perhaps, "Today I give authority to my Highest Self," or "I let my Highest Self lead the way."

We recommend using positive language for your intention statement. So, for a lesson that aims to show you a pattern that is limiting you, such as *Resentment obscures my vision,* come up with an intention overcoming or healing this limitation. In this case, you might write something like, "I let go of resentment and reclaim my vision," or "I release all resentment and allow my vision to be restored."

## Morning Writing

Journaling is good for us. A wide range of studies even back it up. A daily writing practice helps you release and reframe the past; it improves discipline and concentration; it supports goal achievement; it encourages creativity; it enhances self-awareness and emotional intelligence; it promotes physical and psychological healing; and it can even build confidence.

In the Morning Writing section, write a bit about what's coming up for you, your feelings about the day's lesson, an issue you want clarity on, or anything else that asks to be given words. When we identify the *specific words* that comprise our thoughts, a new level of understanding emerges. It's common to feel that you've taken care of something in your mind, only to find that when you write it down, and the *true language* of an inner conflict or desire comes out, that it's not quite what you thought it was. Or it wasn't as "taken care of" as you thought. Writing, especially with a pen on paper, is a powerful means of expression. It joins your voice to your hand, and makes your subjective experience objective – there it is in black and white. Just write.

## Remember

Remember the lesson and your intention throughout the day. Use whatever technology you like to keep yourself engaged with it – sticky notes around your house or workplace, pop-up reminders on your phone or computer, writing it in reverse on your forehead (so it will look normal when you see it in the mirror). Approach the day as a testing ground for applying the lesson.

The more you want freedom, truth, and peace, the more determined you will be to *remember.* And the more actively you remember, pulling yourself out of your dreams and dramas to do this work, the more you will facilitate your transformation.

## Revisit and Reflect

Reflection helps us to learn, grow, and gain perspective. Before bed, revisit the lesson. Think and feel over the day that's coming to a close. Were you able to apply it to your experiences today? How did you feel, act, or perceive things differently than usual? What changed?

Meditate again.

Then, in the Evening Reflections and Gratitude space, record your reflections and write what you're grateful for. A daily gratitude practice can be as transformative as any of the lessons here. This is a great way to bring your blessings to the forefront of your awareness and to let go of the day for a more peaceful night's rest. Finally, ask your Inner Being to integrate the lesson while you sleep.

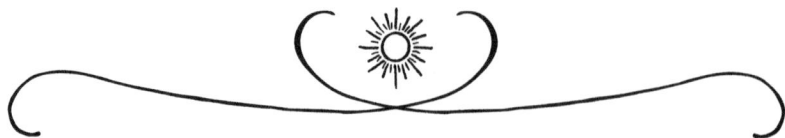

# THE DAILY PROCESS

- As you awaken, first reaffirm your commitment to your Self and this process

- Read the lesson for the day and the explanatory text

- Meditate

- Write freely in the Morning Writing section

- Choose an intention for your day and write it in the Intention section

- Keep your intention in mind throughout the day, and apply the lesson to your circumstances as often as you can

- Before bed, revisit the lesson

- Meditate

- Record your reflections and express gratitude in the Evening Reflections section

- Ask to integrate the lesson while you sleep

- Sleep well

# QUESTIONS AND ANSWERS

**How much time will I need to set aside each day for this?**

Fifteen to thirty minutes each morning and night would be ideal. That will allow you to take your time with the lesson, write at your leisure, let insights arise, and go deep enough in your meditation to reap noticeable benefits.

If you can only spare a few minutes in the morning and a few more at night, you will still benefit from this process, perhaps profoundly. That should give you enough time in the morning to read the lesson, set an intention for the day, and do a moment of meditation (and perhaps to write a few words also). A few minutes should also be enough time in the evening to revisit the lesson, write about what you're grateful for, and take another moment to meditate. However, when additional time is available, few things would be better to invest them in than this course. If you're short on time, the critical factor in your transformation may be whether you prioritize *remembering* throughout the day. This doesn't really demand any *time;* instead it means establishing a habit of making *extra space* and expanding your awareness for the integration of the lesson and your intention.

**What if my partner isn't into it?**

Both you and your partner will benefit from your participation in this process, regardless of whether or not your partner joins you or supports you. Don't do it for them and don't make it about them. Don't let their skepticism or lack of interest fill you with doubt. Evaluate these lessons with your own heart. If your partner seems threatened by your engagement in this work, you can assure them that it's only likely to help you become lighter and happier, and better able to forgive and love them. You can also tell them that the book specifically says you don't have to break up with them in order to become enlightened.

# Why 108 days?

108 is a highly significant number in astronomy, mathematics, martial arts, Hinduism, Buddhism, and more. If you add up the digits of 108 (1+0+8), you get 9, which is associated with abundance or completion, since it's the largest single digit number. 108 is considered to be the number of the Universe, represented by the seed mantra Aum (Om) and the geometric symbol known as the Sri Yantra. It's the number of beads on a mala – the Indian equivalent of a rosary – and therefore the most common number of recitations of mantras. In the Indian astrology system, the sky is divided into 27 regions (*nakshatras*), and if you multiply this number by the four cardinal directions (27x4), you get 108. In Western astrology, we have 12 signs of the Zodiac and 9 planets (12x9=108). Some spiritual traditions view the number 1 as representing God or Truth, 0 as representing emptiness or completeness or the space that contains everything, and 8 as representing infinity or eternity. In Hebrew, the word for life, *chai*, is represented by the numbers 10 and 8.

108 is the measure of the outer angles of a pentacle (five-pointed star) and it's also the measure of the inside angles of a pentagon. Contained within these shapes is the *golden ratio* (expressed by the Greek letter phi – $\Phi$) which is found throughout all lifeforms. The diameter of the Sun is about 108 times the diameter of the Earth. And the average distance of the Sun from the Earth is about 108 Sun-widths. The average distance of the moon from the Earth is about 108 Moon-widths. And if you want something more down-to-earth, 108 is also the number of stitches on a baseball!

We like 108 for all these reasons, but mainly, we had 108 lessons to share and felt it was the right amount of time to ask someone to commit to a practice, and the right amount of time – just over a season – to produce lasting change.

## What if it goes against my religion or personal beliefs?

We're not asking that you join a new religion or that you renounce your existing beliefs. All we ask is that you be open to giving these ideas honest consideration. We want only for you to experience more peace, freedom, and happiness.

Also, in our understanding, we believe the ideas expressed here don't contradict the true essence of any major religion. If you are having difficulty reconciling something you encounter in this book with another belief, meditate on it and ask for clarity.

**I feel bad after having worked on one of these lessons. Why? What should I do?**

It's natural to have some uncomfortable feelings as you reorganize yourself, challenge long-held beliefs, and let go of old patterns and attachments. Think of it as growing pains. There are a number of reasons for this discomfort. One is the echoes of past events as you re-experience and resolve them. Another is that you're feeling the tightness of outdated beliefs that confine you, like becoming aware of the tightness of a pair of shoes as you outgrow them.

A third explanation is that you're experiencing a phenomenon we call "contraction" (which we explain further in lessons 99 and 100). Contraction is a tightening up that often follows a period of personal growth or "expansion." This can happen because you are subconsciously afraid of this new unknown chapter in your life and the release of familiar habits. It can also happen when your ego feels threatened because you've been entering a state of consciousness that seems to make it less important. In a desperate attempt to stay at the forefront of your attention and remain relevant, it generates conflict and negative emotions, hoping that you'll jump back into your ego as your means of navigating this crisis.

Stick with the course. Be kind to yourself. Tell a friend. Get help if you need it. And, most important, forgive yourself. Forgive yourself over and over and over for not always feeling great or for seeming to have backslid. Accept and love yourself regardless of where you are, and remember that you're doing this for your highest good.

**I read a lesson that sounds good in theory, but how would it work if {insert terrible situation here}?**

The simplest advice we can offer is, if you're not currently in such a situation, *don't go there*. "What if" is a device of your anxious mind, pulling you out of the reality of the present and dragging you into the illusion of an unpleasant future. Apply the lesson to *you* and *your* life.

And, if you ever find yourself in {terrible situation} the lessons in this book – *practiced in a sincere, open, and devoted way, with an earnest desire for them to work* – stand to help you more than almost anything else.

**What if I'm too busy?**

Except during *rare* and *extreme* circumstances, we've never encountered anyone who couldn't carve out five minutes each morning and night for something that matters to them.

So, it may be worth asking yourself, *What am I prioritizing instead of this?* And, *What could I do five minutes less of each day?* Checking your email? Hanging out on Facebook? Reading the news?

We know there's a part of you that really wants this. Give it a chance!

**Can I do it again?**

Of course! The next time you do it, you'll inevitably say, "Oh yeah! I needed to hear that again." You'll experience the same lessons differently. You'll peel away more layers and reach new expanses of consciousness, and hopefully new depths of peace, new degrees of freedom, and new heights of happiness.

# A FINAL NOTE

Do it with others and do it with love. We encourage you to join with us and others who are working their way through the book – in our Facebook group *(Rituals for Transformation)*, in conversation, or just in our unified intention.

Even if you live alone, miles from civilization, with no phone or internet, imagine that you're teaming up with millions of others to do the work for everyone, for our collective healing and awakening. And be kind and patient with yourself.

1.

# I AM *grateful* FOR MY *body*

Perhaps your body looks different than you would prefer. Maybe it doesn't quite feel as energetic, comfortable, or youthful as you would like. And it might not always perform as well as you would wish. Perhaps you're in great pain, or disabled, or challenged by severe illness. However, none of these conditions can prevent you from recognizing the gift that your body is.

## THIS BODY DESERVES YOUR GRATITUDE

This body enables you to experience life as a human being. It lets you breathe, drawing the world around you into your lungs. It allows you to see tremendous beauty. To hear the songs of birds, the laughter of children, the whisper of dry leaves. To smell the moist earth, fresh herbs, and a baby's sweet newness. To taste sumptuous foods and your own tears. To touch a feather or another's skin. To build shelters, carry water, dress wounds, and create art.

This body deserves your gratitude. Please take a few minutes today to feel and reflect on what your body has offered. Choose an intention statement regarding how you aim to relate to your body.

*Now Meditate*

# INTENTION
## for the day

☀ MORNING *writing*

☾ EVENING *reflections & gratitude*

2.

# I am NOT my body

You have been judged for your body and you have judged your body. You've fed it. You've exercised it. You've taken it to doctors. You have perhaps abused it at times. You've cleaned it, dressed it, and primped it. Maybe you've tattooed it, dyed its hair, and pierced it. You've paraded it around and used it to do your work. Your body's gender, looks, age, and functionality have shaped your experience of life. At times – perhaps always – it has seemed to be your whole identity. But…

You. Are. Not. Your. Body.

## IT DOESN'T END WHEN THE BODY DIES

Your body doesn't define what you can experience. It cannot limit your capacity for joy or peace. It doesn't dictate your purpose or values or the work you're here to do. And it doesn't restrict your consciousness. What you really are is so much more than the vehicle you utilize, and it doesn't end even when the body dies.

Reflect on how you feel when you believe you are your body, and on how life would be without that belief. Consider an intention that liberates you from any ways in which your identity is limited by your body. As you meditate, allow yourself to perceive just how much more than your body you are.

~ *Now Meditate* ~

# INTENTION
*for the day*

New afrewration
I am we not how
I Look.

## ☀ MORNING *writing*

Beautiful Morning. act as
jesus would have me act.
Feeling as he would feel, Think,
& do.

## ☾ EVENING *reflections & gratitude*

# 3. My BODY IS A VEHICLE for SPIRIT TO EXPERIENCE life

You are so much more than this body and mind, this personality and these circumstances. You are the One Awareness that has chosen to experience life as You. In order to have a truly immersive experience as a human, the Oneness That You Are concealed much of itself from your awareness. Because, how real would all the sorrows and joys feel if you thought you were just playing the part of a human?

## JOYFULLY IMMERSE YOURSELF IN THIS ROLE

Now the Totality of You is being revealed. You'll see that you *are* just playing a part, but this role doesn't need to confine you. As you experience with greater clarity that *what you really are* has nothing to fear, cannot be harmed, and is absolutely loved and cherished, you'll see that you don't need to abandon your human identity in order to be liberated. Instead, while remaining conscious of the fact that you are the Divine Light itself, you can joyfully immerse yourself in this role. And in so doing, you shall awaken others to this reality. In your meditation today, imagine your Highest Self entering and fully enlivening this body.

*Now Meditate*

# INTENTION
## for the day

---

☀ MORNING *writing*

---

☾ EVENING *reflections & gratitude*

---

# 4. I notice the ways in which I WITHOLD APPROVAL from my body

How do you feel when your body doesn't look, feel, or perform as you believe it should? Today, pay attention to your inner criticisms. As the owner of this body, how do you relate to it? What do you say to it? What message are you giving it?

Perhaps you're mostly on good terms – as long as your body works well and looks good. Or maybe you're engaged in a lifelong battle with it, judging, punishing, hating, telling it, "I do not approve of you."

Withholding approval feels like control – as if depriving your body of your love and acceptance will cause it to shape up. You know it doesn't work this way – when you deprive any part of yourself of love, you just feel worse. Maybe you're concerned that if you accept your body as it is, it will never change. But if anything, withholding approval locks your mind and body in a state of conflict that hinders progress.

Today, bring your attention to the ways in which you withhold approval of your body as often as you can. What happens when you look in the mirror? What happens when you catch sight of your skin? What happens when you look down at your frame? What happens when you put on or take off clothes? What happens when you think about aging? When you notice disapproval, feel into it. Whose disapproval is this? How do you experience it? Can you invite the feeling to be here? Can you breathe into it? Can you let it go?

## Now Meditate

# INTENTION
## for the day

☀ MORNING *writing*

☾ EVENING *reflections & gratitude*

# 5. MY BODY SEEMS TO *threaten me* WITH ITS *vulnerability*

If you see your life and consciousness as dependent on your body, this invites a host of other limiting beliefs. This means your body also determines when your life will end. Through its vulnerability, it seems to threaten your vitality and your very existence. It appears to have the power to take away your beauty, your comfort, your functionality, your personality, and your ability to enjoy the world.

## FEEL THE RESENTMENT YOU HOLD AGAINST THIS BODY FOR THREATENING YOU

It's not hard to see how such beliefs might foster an inner war, whereby your body seems a tyrant with endless demands. Today, see if you can feel this conflict. Feel the resentment you hold against this body for threatening you. As you meditate, allow yourself to perceive the nature of this relationship. What would be possible if you were to rise above this conflict and choose peace instead?

*~ Now Meditate ~*

# INTENTION
## for the day

☀ MORNING *writing*

☽ EVENING *reflections & gratitude*

# 6. I *forgive* MY BODY

How would your experience be different if you relinquished all criticisms you hold against your body? How would it feel to accept your body just as it is? What if you could look in the mirror and feel no judgment whatsoever? What if you could stretch and exercise and work, always at peace with whatever feelings might arise? What if you could completely accept the process of getting older? What if you could love your body even when experiencing pain?

## HOW WOULD IT FEEL TO ACCEPT YOUR BODY JUST AS IT IS?

All of this is possible through forgiveness. Today (and always), try to notice any expressions of resistance to your body, and forgive each and every one. Spend a few minutes this morning and night forgiving and releasing layer after layer of judgment, revealing the peace and gratitude that are your native state. And throughout the day, forgive your body as often as you remember.

*Now Meditate*

# INTENTION
## for the day

☀ MORNING *writing*

☾ EVENING *reflections & gratitude*

# 7. I Love my body

As you continue to forgive your body, to express gratitude for your body, and now to love your body fully, consider the sweet sense of ease you could have in this relationship. How much lighter will you feel when any judgment and internal conflict with your body are gone? Let's take it a step further today by actively entering each area of your body with your consciousness, loving it completely and unconditionally. Let there not be a single atom that your love doesn't saturate.

With eyes open or closed, focus on each part of your body and offer it your love. You might even say, "I love you, fingers. I love you, hands. I love you, wrists," and so on. Feel free to move each area, delighting in your body's sophistication and elegance.

After covering all the external structures, imagine each of your organs in turn, and envelop them in love. Some favorites you may wish to include: heart, lungs, liver, kidneys, stomach, spleen, intestines, pancreas, brain, gallbladder. You may also wish to visualize each of the different systems of the body (circulatory, nervous, immune, skeletal, digestive, muscular, etc.), flooding them with love as you do so. Finally, you can imagine your whole collection of trillions of cells, each one lighting up with love, each one relaxing into your total acceptance, your body now full of trillions of microscopic smiles.

*Now Meditate*

# INTENTION
*for the day*

## ☀ MORNING *writing*

## ☾ EVENING *reflections & gratitude*

## 8. I *honor* AND *care* FOR MY *body*

There's a vast difference between caring for your body out of fear versus caring for it out of love. Imagine exercising because you're worried that if you *don't,* you will die or be fat. Now imagine exercising for the sheer delight of fully animating your body.

# CAN YOU LAVISH THIS BODY WITH CARE THE WAY YOU WOULD YOUR OWN CHILD?

When you recognize what a gift this body is, you are inspired to care for it. It is an *honor* to nourish this body. An *honor* to experience and enjoy it, to love it, and to marvel at it. And an *honor* to step into it more consciously, rather than withdrawing from it into your thoughts.

If you could see yourself before your conception, as a soul without a body, who was presented with this amazing vehicle and the opportunity it offers, how could you not treasure it? Without attachment to it, can you lavish this body with care the way you would your own child?

*~ Now Meditate ~*

# INTENTION
*for the day*

## ☀ MORNING *writing*

## ☾ EVENING *reflections & gratitude*

# 9.

# I DELIGHT IN *Moving,* *stretching* AND *working* MY BODY

We live in a unique time when most people in the developed world can live in a way that involves minimal engagement of their body. Probably, you rarely need to chop wood, carry water, or climb trees in the course of managing your everyday life. To make up for the lack of natural exercise in your daily routine, perhaps you have to schedule exercise as a maintenance task. If so, does it feel like a chore? Do you feel guilty when you skip your exercise? Are you concerned that if you don't exercise, it will have negative consequences on your health?

If such feelings are present in your relationship with your body, now is the time to change your perspective. Your body benefits from being moved, worked, and stretched, and it's possible to find delight in each of these activities. Stop exercising out of obligation and figure out where the delight is for you.

Maybe it's in dance. Maybe it's in swimming. Maybe it's in geocaching or adult playgrounds. Maybe it's buried under years of shame. Maybe it's stifled by your resistance to being told what to do. But it's in there, somewhere. When you approach movement this way, you'll start to crave it. The pure joy of inhabiting this body awaits you.

*Now Meditate*

# INTENTION
### for the day

---

☀ MORNING *writing*

---

☽ EVENING *reflections & gratitude*

# 10. *I invite myself to fully experience everything I feel*

With four of your five senses located in your head and a noisy mind clamoring for attention, it's natural to put the majority of your focus on these aspects of your experience, not noticing a large portion of what's available to you. In particular, it's common to miss out on what's happening in your body and the awareness beyond your conscious mind.

## THE PEACEFUL, SILENT 'GROUND' OF YOUR CONSCIOUSNESS IS AVAILABLE TO YOU

Your body is an excellent instrument for registering the presence of conflict or resistance in your mind. Every time you think about controlling some element of your life, every worry, every resentment, every thought that goes against your true, loving nature can be perceived in your body if you just tune in. As you willingly meet these feelings, they can be released. These restrictions can even become learning experiences and portals to greater freedom. Also available to you is the experience of the peaceful, silent "ground" of your consciousness, which becomes easier to access the more you let go of the mental, emotional, and physical "noise" that's been veiling it.

Today, invite yourself to willingly experience everything that is available to you. Bring your consciousness into your body. Into your whole Self.

*Now Meditate*

# INTENTION
## for the day

☀ MORNING *writing*

☾ EVENING *reflections & gratitude*

# 11. I AM NOT MY mind

Even though you've given it a tremendous amount of power and attention; even though you see your mental structures as, in large part, defining your identity; and even though you may consider it one of your most valuable assets . . . you are not your mind.

Your mind is your creation. You were born with a clear and empty mind. Little by little, you began to assemble your experiences into mental constructs you could rely on to help you navigate future situations. With the recognition that your mind was enabling you to get your needs met, and later, to win the approval of your parents, teachers, and peers, and then to manage increasingly complex social situations, you were only too willing to give your mind more of your attention and a greater leadership role.

With each incidence of embarrassment, discomfort, or shame, you had less faith in your ability to manage life without the input of your good friend, Mind. If you're like most people, you've immersed yourself less in your actual experiences and pulled back into the apparent safety of your mind, from where you've formulated calculated behaviors that would be socially acceptable.

Today, remind yourself that you are not your mind. Nor are you the person whose name you use and whose body you occupy. You *have* that person, and you *have* that mind. But you're bigger, freer, and safer than anything your mind can perceive.

~ Now Meditate ~

# INTENTION
## for the day

_____

☀ MORNING *writing*

_____
_____
_____
_____
_____
_____
_____
_____

☾ EVENING *reflections & gratitude*

_____
_____
_____
_____
_____
_____
_____
_____

# 12. I *notice* MY *inner critic*

Like everyone, you have an inner critic. It's the product of an upbringing that emphasized the value of being right, likeable, and approved of. In a confused way, your critic believes it's protecting you by pointing out your flaws. By being your own judgmental parent – or tyrant – you can fix or squelch your "mistakes" before anyone notices. And you can punish yourself for acting, looking, thinking, or feeling imperfectly.

If you've never heard these thoughts, you haven't listened closely enough. While some inner critics are fairly quiet and not terribly mean, we have yet to meet a person who lacked a critic altogether.

The first step to ending this ongoing punishment is noticing it. When the abuse is "below your radar" it's hard to do anything about it. You may simply notice you're not happy, or that you find it difficult to celebrate when you accomplish something, or that there always seems to be something wrong with your circumstances. These may be expressions of the inner degradation being carried out by your mind.

Listen for the words in these negative thoughts today. This requires paying closer attention than usual. Turn up the volume. Perhaps you'll get a sense of your critic's personality and tone of voice. Maybe it sounds like a former teacher, an army sergeant, or a whiny baby. The better you hear its words and recognize its incessant negativity, the more readily you can evaluate its criticisms rather than being silently diminished by them.

*Now Meditate*

# INTENTION
*for the day*

☀ MORNING *writing*

🌙 EVENING *reflections & gratitude*

# 13. I *thank*

## MY MIND FOR ITS EFFORTS TO

# *protect me*

When your mind criticizes you, limits you, and pollutes your experience, it's almost always attempting to protect you – even while it may be destructive in the process. Though the narrow scope of your mind's beliefs may be restrictive, and its few main priorities (such as survival, control, approval, pleasure, and the avoidance of pain) may hinder your evolution, *it believes it's keeping you safe*. The mind doesn't generally respond well to being attacked, so the most effective strategies for managing its tyrannical ways are often gentle ones.

## THE POWERFUL, CLEAR, TIMELESS YOU WILL TAKE IT FROM HERE

Today, practice making space in your consciousness so that you can experience the authority of your Higher Self while observing your mind. Notice the ways your mind attempts to manipulate your perception or grab your attention. And *thank* it.

Treat it like a hyper-vigilant but beloved watch dog. Tell your mind you appreciate that it's always looking out for you, and reassure it that You – the powerful, clear, timeless You – will take it from here. Trust yourself.

*Now Meditate*

# INTENTION
## for the day

☀ MORNING *writing*

☾ EVENING *reflections & gratitude*

# 14. I SEE THE WAYS MY *mind* LIMITS MY *experience* OF LIFE

Your mind is a profound device. It enables you to communicate with other humans, to learn, to solve problems, to create art, and of course, to survive. It takes your survival most seriously (because your survival is *its* survival). Wrapped up in your survival are the pursuits of pleasure, approval, and control (all of which make you feel safe) and the avoidance of pain (which makes you feel endangered). Thus, your mind is always on the lookout for ways to avoid discomfort and threat, and ways to secure more safety, pleasure, approval, and control.

Such an agenda inevitably alters the way you view life. Your mind tries to identify and remember the circumstances that have threatened your safety, and then to recognize these patterns when it sees them again. Except, as marvelous as your mind is, it's imperfect at pattern recognition. So it tends to err on the side of caution – seeing such patterns where they don't actually exist.

This is just one way in which your mind has come to preside over your experience. As it catalogs, analyzes, and critiques, your view is inevitably narrowed. Higher states of consciousness are inaccessible.

Be a witness to your mind's activities today. Without attempting to scold, change, or eliminate the mind, see if you can simply allow your consciousness to expand beyond it, so that you can watch the mind as if from outside it. Are you able to immerse yourself in an experience without looking to your mind for its commentary?

*Now Meditate*

# INTENTION
*for the day*

## ☀ MORNING *writing*

## ☾ EVENING *reflections & gratitude*

# 15. *I forgive my* MIND

## FOR IMPAIRING MY ABILITY TO

# EXPERIENCE
## *peace and happiness*

Despair, fear, anger, sadness, shame, loneliness, and every other negative feeling – they all originate in your mind. You know this. Thus, a part of you sees your mind as having impaired your ability to experience peace and happiness – regardless of whether you feel such feelings are justified.

Forgive your mind today, for any and all ways in which it has degraded your life.

As you meditate, allow yourself to perceive the presence of your thoughts amidst the sea of your awareness and the emotions you carry in your body. Can you see the way they *obscure* your awareness? Can you feel that when you blame or resist your thoughts and emotions, they become stronger, more solid, and more seemingly real? Who would you be if your mind and negative emotions were less substantial, less able to color your lens?

## FORGIVE YOUR MIND TODAY

As you forgive your mind and feelings, over and over, imagine that each successive forgiveness makes them more transparent. Each successive forgiveness loosens the hold your mind and feelings have over you. With each forgiveness, you're released to greater and greater freedom.

### ∽ *Now Meditate* ∽

# INTENTION
*for the day*

## ☀ MORNING *writing*

## ☾ EVENING *reflections & gratitude*

# 16.
# *today*
## I LISTEN WITH
## *my whole self*

Beginning early in childhood, you were taught to place tremendous value on your mind. Your mind produced the right answer that got you praise and approval. Your mind learned how to help you avoid embarrassment and pain, and to ensure your very survival. You trained your mind to produce a continuous stream of analyses and judgments about everything and everyone you encountered. And over time, you learned to listen primarily to your own inner dialogue. That is, your awareness is nearly always dominated by your own thoughts.

## FEEL YOUR PERCEPTION EXPANDING

Today, you'll listen to a vast symphony outside the narrow band of your mind's redundant statements. Let your attention spread beyond your mind. Listen with your body. Listen with your soul. Feel your perception expanding and notice how distant and insignificant the mind's chatter becomes in the context of all that is. What insights await you when you broaden your awareness?

We recommend sitting quietly to practice listening for at least five minutes today. We also encourage you to practice listening more broadly while engaged in conversation, while driving, while working, and in all other activities.

*Now Meditate*

# INTENTION
## for the day

## ☀ MORNING *writing*

## ☾ EVENING *reflections & gratitude*

# 17. I CHOOSE to stay conscious while eating

It is exceedingly common to tune out while eating. We stop paying attention to the fact that we're feeding ourselves and we continue to put food in our mouth on autopilot.

Eating is one of the most special acts you engage in, where you take the most delicious parts of the outside world and incorporate them into yourself. Through this act, you simultaneously nourish your body and reaffirm your unity with the natural world that birthed you and sustains you.

When you go "unconscious," not only is it likely that you'll overeat and under-chew, but you'll also miss out on an opportunity to savor, to feel grateful, to connect with your food, and to perceive how your body is responding to it.

Today, practice staying conscious and connected to the act of eating. Eliminate distractions in order to maximize your enjoyment of this ritual. Choose to eat only at times and places where you *can* devote your consciousness to the act. And when you notice you have tuned out, stop eating, take a breath, recalibrate, ask your body, "Do you want more food?" and listen.

*Now Meditate*

# INTENTION
## for the day

☀ MORNING *writing*

🌙 EVENING *reflections & gratitude*

# 18. I ALLOW
## *Love* AND *Light*
## TO PERMEATE,
## HEAL, AND
## ILLUMINATE ME

You are surrounded by energy. You could call it Love, Light, Qi, Prana, or some other term. It's a fundamental principle of many healing arts, numerous spiritual traditions, and even modern physics. It's what you're made of, and it's always available to you. In your natural state, this energy flows through you in an unrestricted manner, facilitated primarily by the breath. But the flow can be impaired by any of the ways you resist life and argue with reality.

Each day is an opportunity to bask in this light – the very matrix of the universe – to consciously absorb it into every cell of your body. To be energized, purified, and restored by it. And through it, to experience your connection to everything. All you need to do is choose it. Open yourself to it, intend it, and receive it.

Let today be a day of allowing the light to saturate and illuminate you through and through. Imagine that the universe is hugging you from all sides in every moment. Trust that you will be healed. Relax into the arms of the Divine. Let your body, mind, and soul be enveloped in Love.

In today's meditation, give yourself over to this Love and Light. Entertain no thoughts, nor attempt to manipulate your experience – simply let your entire being bask in this gift.

## ~ *Now Meditate* ~

# INTENTION
### for the day

---

☀ MORNING *writing*

---

☾ EVENING *reflections & gratitude*

---

# 19.

## THE WAY
# *I use my words*
## HAS AN
# IMPACT
# *on the world*

Your words have the power to insult and uplift, to hurt and heal. They can degrade your environment or enhance it. Your words have an incalculable resonance. What you choose to communicate – in conversation, writing, tweets, Facebook comments, or any other medium – can affect the recipient more than you know. Their own thoughts, words, and actions may be altered. Those whom *they* encounter may be affected, and so on.

In the same way, the words you think and share today were shaped by generation upon generation of others who came before you. Not just the actual words and the implications ascribed to them over the years, but the thoughts and feelings they carry. They have been directed from person to person, internalized, perhaps distorted, and repeated, in a continuous chain. A distant ancestor might have planted the seed of an internal obstacle you face today by being careless with their words and unintentionally propagating disempowering thoughts and feelings.

Only the most stable and aware people can hear your complaints, fears, and gossip without being affected. Your words shape the internal and external environments that you live in – making them either more or less supportive of your own highest good. Use them wisely.

## ∽ *Now Meditate* ∽

# INTENTION
## for the day

☀ MORNING *writing*

☾ EVENING *reflections & gratitude*

# 20. I *value* MY *inner agreements*

You probably have a sense of the repercussions of breaking your agreements with others: anger, disappointment, loss of trust, damage to the relationship. But what happens when you break an agreement with yourself? Chances are, you let yourself off the hook and don't think much more of it.

But those agreements with yourself are every bit as important as the ones you make with others. And the impact of keeping them – or breaking them – affects your whole life. When you don't honor your word with the one closest to you (you), you lose trust in yourself. Your sense of yourself is diminished. You weaken the power of your word. You feed your inner critic. You undermine your ability to accomplish ambitious goals. And you give yourself the message, *I don't respect you; you don't matter.*

You can't hide from yourself or trick yourself into believing you didn't really mean it when you made the agreement. Even if the agreement was never written down, if you set a clear intention in your mind, there will be some form of damage if you don't honor your words and your creative power.

Begin valuing your inner agreements, and thus valuing you. Forgive yourself for all the agreements you've broken with yourself. Only make agreements you know you can keep. And make a sacred contract with yourself to value your agreements with yourself from here on out. (That doesn't mean that you won't ever break an agreement with yourself again, it just means that when you do, you'll acknowledge it and clean it up with yourself.) Throughout each day, notice the agreements you're making, and write them down so they are not vague or easily forgotten, and keep them, as you would keep them with your best friend.

*∽ Now Meditate ∽*

# INTENTION
## for the day

☀ MORNING *writing*

☾ EVENING *reflections & gratitude*

# 21. MY *agreements* ARE LIKE *Seeds* IN THE *world*

As you consistently keep your agreements with yourself and others, you build your power and develop momentum. When you always do what you say you're going to do, you dependably turn intention into reality. Day after day, you state the truth before it happens. The universe knows how to support such an individual.

Moreover, when you keep your agreements, your mind settles down. It is less likely to obstruct the delivery of the circumstances you request because it already knows it can trust you to follow through on what you set forth.

## WHEN YOU KEEP YOUR AGREEMENTS, YOUR MIND SETTLES DOWN

Like any good gardener, you don't simply scatter seeds and walk away. You enrich the soil over years by honoring your environment and keeping your word. You dig holes for your seeds by feeling into yourself to ensure that your agreements are aligned with your heart. You water and shine your light on your seedlings by giving your agreements your enthusiastic presence. And you pull the weeds around them by withdrawing your energy from distractions that compromise your focus.

*Now Meditate*

# INTENTION
*for the day*

## ☀ MORNING *writing*

## ☾ EVENING *reflections & gratitude*

# 22. I CHOOSE TO BE

## *intentional*

## AROUND MAKING

## *agreements*

Clarity around agreements is an essential part of building trust in yourself and honoring your word. Ambiguity makes for a weak foundation. If you aren't crystal clear, you may not know how to fulfill an agreement. You may not even know if you *have* an agreement.

Keep a clean mind. Define for yourself what exactly constitutes an agreement. Bring your consciousness to every new agreement. Make sure it's something you can earnestly devote yourself to and that you fully intend to keep. Don't make an agreement if your heart's not in it.

## BRING YOUR CONSCIOUSNESS TO EVERY NEW AGREEMENT

Finally, being intentional with your agreements means treating them not as mere obligations but opportunities to enthusiastically demonstrate your integrity and the power of your word.

*Now Meditate*

# INTENTION
## for the day

## ☀ MORNING *writing*

## ☾ EVENING *reflections & gratitude*

# 23. I USE *my* WORDS *with* CARE

Your words, whether written, spoken aloud, or held in your mind, color your experience of life and influence your environment. All day, every day, the words that form your inner dialogue and the ones with which you talk about your past, present, and future create the story you live. Whether this is a tragedy or a triumph depends in large part on the script you choose.

The moment you change the script, you change your experience. And as your community witnesses this change, it changes, too. It becomes an environment that nourishes and supports your Highest Self.

Further, your words are the means by which you express your intentions and agreements. They are the foundation of your integrity, the basis of self-trust, and a powerful tool of creation.

Pay special attention to the words you use. How do you characterize your past? Your current challenges? Your future? How do you speak of others? Of the world? What is the impact of your words in your conversations? If you post or comment on social media, do your words uplift or degrade? Do you talk more about what's wrong or what's good? Do you point out problems or offer solutions? Finally, what happens when you choose your words with care? What happens when you use words that are aligned with Truth and Love?

*Now Meditate*

# INTENTION
## for the day

---

☀ MORNING *writing*

---

☾ EVENING *reflections & gratitude*

# 24. *I take time for* STILLNESS *today and every day*

Our minds are more active than ever, occupied always in stimulation, absorption, analysis, judgment, and rehashing. Computers, cell phones, televisions, books, magazines, newspapers – an infinite supply of media enable us to be constantly engaged. Information consumption is an addiction and an epidemic. Meanwhile, deliberate mental stillness is a rare and special thing.

## LET YOUR MIND RECEDE INTO THE BACKGROUND

In stillness there is peace and connection. There is the sense that *this, right now, is enough*. Stillness is healing to a mind that has forgotten how to be present and focused. In stillness you remember that there is nothing wrong. In stillness you can perceive the *timeless ground* of reality.

Today, let yourself happily dedicate some of your time to stillness. Take as much time as you're willing, as often as you can, to *hold space* in your consciousness for stillness. Make these moments an offering to Awareness. See how long you can refrain from filling this space with thoughts. Let your mind recede into the background. When you notice you're following a thought train, gently bring yourself back. If you need something to focus on, simply watch yourself breathe.

*Now Meditate*

# INTENTION
## *for the day*

☀ MORNING *writing*

☾ EVENING *reflections & gratitude*

# 25. Forgiveness
## is the key to freedom

All the ways in which your inner and outer world are unacceptable to you represent the degree to which you are constrained. If life were a map of the world, the people you disdain, the aspects of your personality that don't meet your approval, and the unforgiven events of your past would be like territories you've decided are off limits. While you may tell yourself you're happy to live in the remaining regions where you're comfortable, when you're ready for complete freedom – a deeper peace, and greater happiness, you'll need to visit these places and forgive them.

In truth, a map is not a personal enough metaphor. Your condemnation of these facets of life is more like refusing to use a painful leg. This may lessen your exposure to the pain, but it comes at the expense of your own mobility. Imagine how different life would be if you suddenly regained the use of a limb that was paralyzed. Forgiveness works this way. In the moment of forgiveness, freedom and untapped capacities are restored.

Every time you forgive it's like clearing a clog in the stream of life that pours through you. Like thinning the viscous fluid you've been moving through. Like dropping the sandbags that have been weighing you down. Or like snipping the ropes that have kept you tethered.

When you forgive the world completely you give yourself permission to be whomever you are. With forgiveness, locked doors are unlocked. Dark rooms are illuminated. Scattered fragments of your power are reclaimed. Estranged relations are reunited. There's no place you can't go.

## ~ Now Meditate ~

# INTENTION
## for the day

_____
_____
_____

## ☀ MORNING *writing*

_____
_____
_____
_____
_____
_____
_____
_____

## ☾ EVENING *reflections & gratitude*

_____
_____
_____
_____
_____
_____
_____

# 26.
# *I am limited*
# *by* WITHOLDING
# *forgiveness*

The objects of your withheld forgiveness are not just the perpetrators of obvious crimes, like the people who have hurt you – they also include all the facets of your inner and outer world that you don't completely accept. Not accepting them turns them into impediments and inhibits the flow of life through you. As a river of experience passes through your awareness, you pick out the things you dislike and say, "No. This I don't accept." It burdens you with an ongoing discomfort and impairs your freedom.

## COULD I LET ALL OF THIS GO?

Notice all of your complaints with the world and yourself. Notice all the ways in which you don't accept the world exactly as it is. Notice all the possible outcomes for the future that you seek to prevent. All the ways in which the weather doesn't line up with your plans, and humans disappoint you. And *feel* the constraint that this causes. Today, just become aware of how restricted your experience is and ask yourself, could I let all of this go? Could I forgive instead of seeking to restrict?

*Now Meditate*

# INTENTION
## for the day

## ☀ MORNING *writing*

## ☾ EVENING *reflections & gratitude*

# 27.

# Resentment

## O B S C U R E S

# my vision

When you harbor resentment, it dims your vision. It narrows your perspective. And it shrinks your possibilities. Instead of a world of limitless options, you see the ways in which things aren't quite right. While open eyes would perceive beauty, diversity, and innocence, eyes narrowed by resentment see brokenness, separation, and deceit.

Your resentment trains you to see evidence of your rightness. The more you perceive the world as confirming this, the deeper your illusion. It's as if all of creation is depicted in a massive painting – a mural a mile long. If you were to step back far enough to take the whole thing in, it would take your breath away. You would see infinite expressions of Love.

But instead of this perspective, you have found the one small corner of the painting that depicts confusion and pain, and you don't like it. Your dislike won't change the painting, of course. Instead, it prevents you from stepping back and understanding. Here you sit, staring at that minuscule part of the Whole, unhappy and insisting that it shouldn't be this way.

Let it go and discover again your capacity to see the big picture, to understand the Truth. When you choose to see beyond your resentment, your experience will be of awe and gratitude. Rather than fixating on what appears to be wrong, you'll perceive the context, and you'll trust and grow.

## Now Meditate

# INTENTION
*for the day*

## ☀ MORNING *writing*

## ☾ EVENING *reflections & gratitude*

# 28. Forgiveness is an ONGOING Commitment

As much as you might hope that you can make a momentary expression of forgiveness and then forever be free, your mind may not comply with this desire. Strong feelings cut deep grooves and minds easily fall back into them. Therefore, true forgiveness must be a commitment. A sincere, heartfelt commitment to be vigilant, to notice when your resentment has returned, and to forgive again. It's a commitment to maintain the spirit of active forgiveness until there's no longer an acute need for it. And even when the resentment seems forever gone, if it rears its head decades later you will continue to forgive – without judgment or self-flagellation.

## WHAT COMPLAINTS DO I COMMIT TO FORGIVE NOW AND FOREVER?

Forgiving isn't a task to be done and checked off your to-do list. It's a state you embody, a presence that you bring into your life and continuously apply to your interactions, your past mistakes, others' mistakes, and whatever you judge in family members, politicians, media figures, corporations, and literally everyone and everything else.

In your meditation today, ask yourself, "What complaints do I *commit* to forgive now and forever?"

*Now Meditate*

# INTENTION
## for the day

☀ MORNING *writing*

☾ EVENING *reflections & gratitude*

# 29. FORGIVENESS *transcends* TIME AND SPACE

When you forgive, time and space collapse. The unforgiven condemnation of the past lives today in all the minds that subscribe to it. But as you forgive the past, it changes. Healing is delivered to an age-old wound. A story of sin is rewritten. As the past is released, the present and future change as well. And because the past and future live always in the present, when you forgive the present, all of time is altered.

Space, too, folds upon itself to deliver the light of your pardon. As you release the most distant constraint in your mind, light spreads across the universe, illuminating any pockets that were previously condemned to darkness.

## WHEN YOU FORGIVE, TIME AND SPACE COLLAPSE

True forgiveness is an earthly expression of the Divine, which is beyond time and space. It sheds light on a dream of separation and in so doing, restores unity. Both forgiver and forgiven are blessed by this process.

In your meditation, see if you can transcend the structures of time and space as you allow the light of forgiveness to fill your heart. Forgive, whether the object of your forgiveness is here or there, whether it's now or then or later, and notice how the world becomes the heaven it always was.

*Now Meditate*

# INTENTION
*for the day*

## ☀ MORNING *writing*

## ☾ EVENING *reflections & gratitude*

# 30. I *heal* MY *wounds*

## WITH FORGIVENESS

Unhealed wounds can be easily reopened. They can cause you great pain if they're poked. They present an ongoing vulnerability that detracts from your freedom and resilience. It is worthwhile to discover any such wounds in yourself. Not so that they can be forgotten, or so that you can pretend they never happened, but so that you can experience freedom in their presence, so they no longer exist as vulnerabilities and limitations.

There is one salve that works on all wounds, from the shallowest to the deepest, from the most recent to the oldest. It heals the wounds that seem to be yours personally and those that you share with humanity. This salve is forgiveness.

Apply it liberally and repeatedly to any wounds, whether they seem to be yours or someone else's, whether they're fresh or old, whether they seem insurmountable or so minor as to be insignificant. Apply forgiveness to all of these, so they can be healed over with new skin. Sometimes a scar will remain to remind you of what you've overcome.

*Now Meditate*

# INTENTION
## for the day

---

## ☀ MORNING *writing*

---

## ☾ EVENING *reflections & gratitude*

# 31. MY *purpose* TODAY IS TO *enhance* MY ENVIRONMENT

What could be possible if you were to align yourself with this purpose? As soon as you make this choice, you'll see opportunities – in every conversation and every interaction with the world. It's like walking into a coloring book with a set of brilliantly colored markers. It is a challenge that never gets old, a perpetual outlet for the expression of your artistry. Not only do you get the satisfaction of beautifying these scenes, you also get to reside in them.

When you consciously choose the purpose of enhancing your environment, you'll inevitably begin to notice your tendencies to taint it. In your social environment, you'll see yourself wanting to complain, wanting to arouse anger and outrage, wanting to enroll others in your fears, resisting reality and mirroring others' resistance back to them, and supporting friends to live in illusion. In your physical environment, you'll become more aware of the impact of your consumption, and your personal legacy of waste on the planet. In your psychological environment, you will see your habits of indulgence in negative thoughts and feelings. If you're tempted to beat yourself up for these behaviors, don't – that would be more degradation. Instead, remember your purpose and do what you can. Don't underestimate your impact.

Tell yourself, as often as you remember, "My purpose today is to enhance my environment."

*Now Meditate*

# INTENTION
## for the day

☀ MORNING *writing*

🌙 EVENING *reflections & gratitude*

# 32. RESISTANCE IS THE fundamental human pathology

The most basic departure from health occurs through *resistance*. Far simpler than malnutrition or infection is the inner expression of "No." We experience discomfort and we resist the experience.

Not all resistance is pathological. Early in life, this discomfort was associated with unmet needs – for milk, for warmth, for comfort, for connection – and your resistance was made clear to your caregivers, who probably responded by guessing at these needs and doing their best to address them. At other times you momentarily resisted a taste or touch or smell you disliked. It was a visceral aversion to something unpleasant; perhaps it even saved your life.

But as you got older, the objects of your resistance grew in number and became more diverse and complicated. You learned to resist people, emotions, beliefs, images, memories, and ideas – whether present or not, real or not. You shaped your path and personality not just by your interests and expressions, but by the things you resist.

Deep down, beneath conscious thought, perhaps you resist your own personality, or your humanness, or the feeling of inhabiting this body, or the experience of having a mind that doesn't know everything and perhaps berates you, or the feeling of being disconnected from your Source.

Today, simply attempt to recognize your resistance. Bring something to mind that you wish were different about your life and feel what comes up in your body. Think of a person you dislike and feel what your body does. Get to know this feeling. It's usually a bracing, hardening, closing, or clenching. Sometimes it's right at the surface, glaring and obvious. Other times it's so subtle or so *familiar* you may not even realize it's there. Perhaps it's part of how you *always* feel. Today, be curious about it and bring it to the light.

*~ Now Meditate ~*

# INTENTION
## for the day

☀ MORNING *writing*

☾ EVENING *reflections & gratitude*

# 33. I *release*
## ANY RESISTANCE TO WHAT I FEEL

Nearly all resistance is founded in confusion. It comes from the impulsive thought that if you resist something it will get better or go away. It's a reflex that rarely benefits you and often magnifies your discomfort. Moreover, it gives power to your ego and it reinforces the sense that you're a small, disconnected human, at the mercy of the world.

Resistance tends to produce stagnation. Clenching and closing impede the flow of life through us. And stagnation is uncomfortable. (All pain has at its root some form of stagnation.) When we resist something uncomfortable, the resistance this causes *compounds* the discomfort, and we respond with more resistance. It can be a difficult cycle to end.

Imagine that a big hose passes through you, entering your back and coming out through your chest. Passing through the hose is the full spectrum of life experience. People, interactions, stories, journeys, conflict, triumph . . . and whenever something you dislike moves through you, you reflexively tense up, squeezing around the hose. You don't want it to pass through you. But in effect, you've halted it within yourself. You're *holding it*. This is the meaning of the expression, "What you resist persists." When you resist feeling thoughts, emotions, physical sensations, and experiences that are uncomfortable, they become compartmentalized pockets of darkness, part of your shadow self. If you don't acknowledge and integrate these facets of yourself, they limit your freedom.

If what you resist persists, then *a feeling fully felt finally fades*. If you feel willingly and without resistance, experiences move through you without becoming knots. Also, as today's experiences evoke memories of past experiences, you have an opportunity to release persistent snarls that have restricted you for many years. Rather than resisting, invite each uncomfortable experience to open, allow it to be felt with your whole self. Without resistance, the ego loses power over us.

*Now Meditate*

# INTENTION
## for the day

---

☀ MORNING *writing*

---

☾ EVENING *reflections & gratitude*

# 34. RESISTANCE
## WILL NEVER IMPROVE MY
# *feelings*
## OR
# *circumstances*

Although it's possible to take action and change circumstances or feelings that you resist, your resistance itself is not the agent of such change. In fact, your resistance impedes transformation. To the degree that you refuse to accept the reality of your experience, you lock up your energy.

This doesn't mean that you should never say *no*. You may be tempted to indulge in negative thinking or to do things that would be bad for your health. People may attempt to harm you. In these cases, a clear *No* is likely your best response. But once you've made your choice, you'll be best served by accepting the present circumstances – *this is what's happening* – and acting in support of this choice.

Notice how it feels when you resist your own thoughts or feelings. By comparison, what happens when you integrate what you have rejected? What happens when you drop the fight? If you feel called to act for change, act. But can you can remain *open* while acting? Can you do it without attachment to personal gain? And finally, can you do it without denying the Love that is your true nature?

*Now Meditate*

# INTENTION
## for the day

☀ MORNING *writing*

☾ EVENING *reflections & gratitude*

# 35. I *feel* THE WAYS I *resist* LIFE AND I *let go*

Throughout every day, there are countless things you may resist: waking up, aches in your body, unpleasant news, feeling that you should have exercised or meditated but didn't, slow traffic, a coworker's body odor, your tiredness, the amount of money you have, the work you have to do, and anything else that you want to be different than it is.

Every one of these thoughts of resistance goes along with a feeling in your body. If you bring your awareness to your body while holding such a thought, you'll learn to perceive a certain tension. Most of us have favorite places we habitually clench as a physical expression of our resistance.

As you go through your day, as often as possible – and especially during any moment of conflict or aversion – feel what comes up in your body. Allow yourself to experience it, to learn what's inside it. See what it reveals. And let it go.

*Now Meditate*

# INTENTION
## for the day

☀ MORNING *writing*

☾ EVENING *reflections & gratitude*

# 36. MY *energy* AND *attention*

## ARE TREMENDOUSLY VALUABLE

What you feed with your energy and attention grows. They are the lifeforce that nurtures your intentions. They have the power to change lives – your own and others. Channeled into creative endeavors, they'll produce beauty and utility. Directed into healing, they will bolster vitality. Brought to bear upon a problem, they will uncover solutions. Offered to your work, they will yield satisfaction and productivity.

Honor these powers by choosing consciously to what or whom they are given.

If your intention is to deliver these powers to a chosen focus, observe whether or not you're actually doing so. If you mean to give your attention and energy to your relationship, for instance, notice if they're instead being poured into the meanderings of your mind, your electronic devices, or some other unacknowledged priority.

## WHAT YOU FEED WITH YOUR ENERGY AND ATTENTION GROWS

Whatever you may believe your priorities to be, the things that get your energy and attention are your *true* priorities, and you'll see this manifest in the state of your life.

*Now Meditate*

# INTENTION
### *for the day*

☀ MORNING *writing*

☾ EVENING *reflections & gratitude*

# 37. Resistance

## OBSTRUCTS

## my ENERGY

If you want to experience more energy or a greater sense of ease in your life, it's vital to recognize the role that resistance plays in thwarting both of these.

Resistance – regardless of what you're resisting – can make you feel tired, mentally unclear, and uneasy. While each person's bodily experience of resistance is different – as a tightness, an ache, a feeling of jitteriness, etc. – all of these different sensations are a kind of *unease*. And not only does this impede the free flow of energy, it also consumes energy to maintain this inner state of tension.

Resistance is also present when you don't *trust*. When you don't trust yourself or the universe, you tend to clench, close, bear down, put up your armor, and attempt to control your environment, all of which further squelches the free flow of energy through you. It tends to have a *contractive* influence on your mind and body, which naturally impairs the effective storage and utilization of energy. Imagine dancing, writing, running, counseling, or giving a speech in each of two states – first, in a state of tension and resistance; second in a state of acceptance and ease.

If you're uncertain of how to proceed, feel into your body and ask yourself, "What am I resisting?" Whatever comes up . . . breathe into it, listen to it, and release it.

## ～ Now Meditate ～

# INTENTION
## for the day

☀ MORNING *writing*

☾ EVENING *reflections & gratitude*

# 38. All THE Energy I NEED IS available TO ME

In both ancient medical systems and modern physics, the world is understood to be composed at its most fundamental level of *energy*. It's what we're made of, it's in the air we breathe, the sun that shines upon us, the water we drink, and the food we eat. Matter is energy. Light is energy. Love is energy. Changing your experience of energy begins with a change of perspective.

If you find yourself *chasing* energy, try making yourself *open* to it instead. Imagine an open column like a vertical axis through your body, running from the top of your head to the bottom of your pelvis. Imagine this column has a magnetism that pulls energy into itself, like pure white light, from every direction, especially from the sky above you into the top of the column and from the earth below you into the bottom of the column. You can also imagine an openness in every cell of your body, and a readiness to *receive* the abundant energy that surrounds you.

Like the Sun, the Divine does not withhold energy. Your every interaction with the world presents an opportunity to be nourished and energized. A single deep breath, inhaled with total conviction of the power within it, can change your energy in an instant. What if you practiced such awareness with every breath, every bite of food, every sip of water, every touch of sun or soil upon your skin, every hug, every gaze at the majesty of the world around you? You would be transformed.

*Now Meditate*

# INTENTION
## for the day

☀ MORNING *writing*

☾ EVENING *reflections & gratitude*

## 39.

# I BECOME *aware*

## OF HOW ENERGY

# *Comes* TO ME

## AND *leaves* ME

In an age when humans so often seek *stimulation* – to have our energy aroused or augmented – it's worthwhile to become aware of how your energy is depleted and replenished. The main way this is accomplished is by paying attention. When you make a regular practice of expanding your awareness beyond your mind, perceiving the ups and downs of your energy is entirely possible.

What drains your energy? What fills you up?

When your energy is low, notice how you're breathing. What happens if you breathe more deeply and fully? Notice your relationship with what you're engaged in or whom you're engaged with. What happens if you consciously refrain from "leaking" your energy into it, instead consolidating your energy in your core while continuing the task or conversation? What happens if you choose to participate with full consent, expecting to be inspired and delighted by what you'll find? What happens if you pretend you're playing a game rather than making life all serious?

Learn how your energy is depleted and replenished and you'll know how to live a long, balanced, and spirited life.

### ∼ *Now Meditate* ∼

# INTENTION
## for the day

☀ MORNING *writing*

☾ EVENING *reflections & gratitude*

# 40.

# Within my resistance is an *untrue story*

Of the many different things you resist – thoughts, feelings, people, places, tasks, changes – there's a consistent story beneath most of this resistance. It goes something like this:

*I don't (or can't) accept this. If I resist, it will get better or go away. If I stop resisting, something bad will happen or the thing I dislike will become worse.*

99 times out of 100, this story will confine you, stunt your growth, make you feel like a victim, and close you to the truth. You don't need to resist to survive.

From the big view, it doesn't matter whether you resist or don't resist. You'll have a tremendous human experience and eventually reunite with your Source. So why not allow this experience to be one of ease and enjoyment?

Let go – of the resistance *and* the story – and see what happens.

*Now Meditate*

# INTENTION
## for the day

---

☀ MORNING *writing*

---

☾ EVENING *reflections & gratitude*

# 41.

## I forgive myself

### FOR ANY WAY IN WHICH I HAVE

## obstructed

### MY OWN

## happiness AND potential

One of the many things we are likely to blame ourselves for is the belief that if we had done things differently or had been a different kind of person, we would be happier or more successful today. We believe we have obstructed our own happiness and potential in some way. Perhaps when you look back, you think, "I spent so much time being unhappy when I could've been happy" or, "I could have done so much more."

Even if it's true that you spent much of your past oblivious to how much you had to be grateful for, even if it's true that you could be more successful or wealthy today if you had thought or acted differently, it's time to release this self-blame and forgive yourself anyway.

It may also be worthwhile to reframe the way you think about yourself, to change the script of the story you tell yourself. If nothing else, forgive yourself because continued punishment wastes energy, degrades your consciousness, cuts you off from Love, and further stifles your potential.

But to take it further, try this on. In the big picture of who you are and why you're here, you can do no wrong. You are here to play. To experience. And any healing that occurs along the way is a bonus to all. Any light you can bring to the world is appreciated. Any kindness you can offer to the confused masses is welcomed. So be grateful that you are *here now*. Regardless of what was done and how you have felt up until now, you can change this very moment. Don't let the past dictate your present. Forgive. Let go. Be free.

## Now Meditate

# INTENTION
*for the day*

## ☀ MORNING *writing*

## ☾ EVENING *reflections & gratitude*

# 42. Today I turn toward whatever I resist

When something feels unpleasant, you tend to be repelled. It's natural, in the same way that you reflexively pull your hand away from a hot pan. But when that unpleasant feeling is within you, pulling away from it impedes its resolution. If you try to pull away from *yourself,* you only cause inner conflict and fragmentation.

Retreating from discomfort tends to magnify the unpleasant feeling, because in pulling away from it you seem to be telling yourself that it can't be faced or figured out. And yet it's within you, like being stuck with a repulsive cellmate. Your aversion to feeling what's coming up turns a transient experience into a compartmentalized *problem.*

What happens when you instead turn *toward* what you resist? It may feel counterintuitive at first. But chasing pleasure and avoiding pain is the compulsion of the most primitive, animalistic part of you. It's time to evolve past these survival instincts.

Instead, allow yourself to rediscover your innate curiosity and bravery. Then you'll find yourself *wanting* to know and feel what's in those places, feelings, and circumstances you avoid. You'll experience increased freedom and understanding from every meeting. And turning away will begin to feel like putting off the inevitable.

Turn toward what you resist and look more closely. See what's really inside. The problem may be less substantial than you believe. Turn toward it so that you can heal and no longer be manipulated by this. Turn toward and integrate what you've rejected in yourself and the world.

*Now Meditate*

# INTENTION
*for the day*

## ☀ MORNING *writing*

## ☾ EVENING *reflections & gratitude*

# 43. *Everything is perfect*

You can tune in to a variety of different channels of perception, such as outrage or everything-is-perfect.

To a person hanging out in the outrage channel, the very idea of someone holding the perspective that everything is perfect is, of course, an outrage. But from the everything-is-perfect perspective, everything, including the outraged person, is perfect.

You emerged from perfection. The only difference between you and your Source is that your perception is limited. You're accustomed to seeing life through a keyhole, and you tend to judge the whole based on your microscopic viewpoint. Your human mind may be incapable of grasping the Totality, but your consciousness is certainly capable of perceiving the Oneness That You Are – and its perfection.

If you view life from the perspective of "The world has lots of problems," then of course, you'll see problems everywhere. Perhaps you believe you're just calling what's broken, broken. But are you sure you're not seeing an imperfect world as a consequence of your own pronouncement that it's imperfect? What if you suspend judgement for the moment? Can you know with absolute certainty that in the big scheme of things, there is an error in the emergence of the universe? What exactly constitutes imperfection? And who gets to decide that *something that is*, is wrong? Are you sure your mind is the authority here? Can you be innocent? Can you be humble?

You have the choice of consciously selecting your perspective. If you've given your mind the authority to declare the world imperfect, it must also have the authority to declare it perfect. Look at your world with the perspective that it's perfect – all of it – and you'll see a perfect world.

You'll still have times when strong emotion contracts your consciousness around some dramatic thought. And why not revel in the delicious theatrical roller coaster of it? Just remember that, even if you can't access that perspective of perfection, it's still perfect.

*Now Meditate*

# INTENTION
## for the day

☀ MORNING *writing*

☾ EVENING *reflections & gratitude*

# 44.
## I go with the flow

Being in the flow is your natural state. Life has trajectories, like the movement of water in a river. There are easier and harder ways to get things accomplished, by going with or against the current.

Going with the flow doesn't mean conforming to what society wants you to do, or avoiding work, or sidestepping challenges. Choose your path based on the calling of your soul and the knowing in your heart – even if it means hard labor, even if it threatens deeply held beliefs, even if it is the greatest challenge you've ever faced. And once you've made this choice, follow through with it by choosing to stay *in the flow,* and you will be rewarded with a sense of ease, even while there's sweat on your brow.

Going with the flow entails learning to perceive the current and to feel when you're paddling against it. The *true current* has nothing to do with social or economic pressures. You can choose an unpopular path and still be in the flow. Learn to feel the contours of life and the physics of movement.

Going with the flow lets you harness the momentum around you to get more done with less. It means, at times, not being the *doer* at all. Mostly it takes only gentle guidance, a subtle shift of the rudder to choose one path or another, as you continue to glide along. The more you learn to perceive the flow and allow yourself to move with it, the greater will be your experience of ease and trust.

*Now Meditate*

# INTENTION
## for the day

## ☀ MORNING *writing*

## ☾ EVENING *reflections & gratitude*

# 45. I FORGIVE MYSELF for not always BEING STRONG

You have felt weak at times. You have given in to temptation. You have buckled under the pressures of life. You have been unable to do it all yourself, unwilling to come face-to-face with your fears, afraid to speak up, or incapable of handling the pain. And probably, you have blamed yourself for this.

We all have cycles. Like day becoming night and summer becoming fall, the balance of nature means energy cannot be always at its peak. Your capacities wax and wane. Accept where you are and forgive yourself for not being strong in every moment. Look back at the times you have criticized yourself for being weak and rewrite those stories.

## ACCEPT WHERE YOU ARE

It's important that you also understand that while the strength of your mind and body are inconsistent, that of your Highest Self is constant. If you find yourself cowering from life, spending your days in hiding, compromising your experience of life, or letting timidity undermine your purpose, first forgive yourself. Then, open yourself to the Divine courage and strength that are always available to you.

~ Now Meditate ~

# INTENTION
## for the day

☀ MORNING *writing*

☾ EVENING *reflections & gratitude*

# I trust myself to MANAGE whatever life brings me

You don't need to control all the details. Choose the kind of life you want. Make the best plans you can. Keep your agreements. And trust.

You have the resources to manage this life. You have always managed. Even if you've sometimes broken down. Even if you've sometimes freaked out. Even if you've sometimes needed help. Here you are today, still managing.

There's nothing bigger than the Totality of what you are. You've mistakenly identified yourself as merely the small character who's living your life, but you're much more than that. You're connected and whole and in that, you're capable, steadfast, and strong.

You are held and loved by your own Highest Self. Peace is always within you, beneath the noise. Strength is yours to access whenever you need it. You can never truly fail at this game.

Trust yourself.

*Now Meditate*

# INTENTION
## for the day

_____

☀ MORNING *writing*

_____

_____

_____

_____

_____

_____

_____

☾ EVENING *reflections & gratitude*

_____

_____

_____

_____

_____

_____

_____

# 47. I am a child of nature ~ We are forever connected

While it's easy to regard Nature as merely the *stuff* that surrounds your life, to do so means missing out on a deeply important connection. Nature is your Creator. Numerous spiritual traditions refer to the earth as Mother and the sky as Father. And whether or not you relate to the earth as female and the heavens as male, the *relationship* they speak of is real and it's always available to you.

You were birthed from and of Nature. Everything you eat, all the people and objects you interact with, the air you breathe, the water you drink – *all* of it originated in the natural world. Nature feeds you, houses you, it provides everything your life revolves around, and yet, in the midst of it, it's still possible to have a vague, mostly pleasant, but disconnected sense of it. Like the affectionate way you feel about National Geographic.

It's literally your *everything,* and yet, you tend to focus on individual pieces of it with rarely a conscious experience of the cohesiveness of it all – the fact that it is *All One.* Including you.

You may not perceive it, but it breathes with you. It moves with you. It has a rhythm that you're a part of. The more time you spend in consciousness of this connection, the stronger it gets. And your soul *yearns* for it. It's like having ignored your mother for most of your life, even though you interact on a daily basis with her fingers and toes. Your heart aches to reconnect. And when you do, you just feel right...at home.

~ Now Meditate ~

# INTENTION
### for the day

## ☀ MORNING *writing*

## ☾ EVENING *reflections & gratitude*

# 48.

# When I harbor RESENTMENTS of the world, I am not seeing the whole TRUTH

Each vision you attempt to superimpose upon the world is like a hazy lens laid over your own eyes. You can be sure that as long as you believe the world should be different than it is, the truth will remain hidden from you. The farther the world is from the way you believe it should be, the farther you are from living in Truth. And the crux of this discrepancy lies in your resentments.

Your resentments keep you from seeing what's really there. They obscure the unity of all things. They encourage you to construct your identity around but a fraction of what you really are.

Relinquishing your resentments is like cataract surgery. The cloudy veil removed, you are able to see and awaken to the reality of your divinity and that of the world. When you allow the world to be exactly as it is, the truth emerges; and when the truth emerges, you see the arrogance of believing the world imperfect.

The time is now to clear the murk. You're being called to let go of your resentment, to use the gift of forgiveness to change the direction of your life, to see Oneness, and to open your heart to allow Spirit its rightful home. Throughout the day, notice when you're resenting and choose something else.

*Now Meditate*

# INTENTION
## for the day

## ☀ MORNING *writing*

## ☾ EVENING *reflections & gratitude*

# 49. I forgive myself FOR MY anger

Today, notice all of your anger. The anger that's easy to access and the anger that has been suppressed. Today, don't be afraid to feel it. Here is the day to experience it fully so that it and you can be mutually released.

Today is the day to get to know this feeling. So it can't control you, so it can't alter your behavior without your awareness. Today is the day to know it so well that it's not your boss anymore. You no longer react to it like an animal. Today is the day to look into it, to feel into it, to dive into its core, to feel it thoroughly. Without shame or embarrassment. Evaluate it impartially. Neutrally. There are things you like about it. What are they? There are things you dislike about it. What are they?

How has anger caused you to act against your values? How has anger caused you to sacrifice your inner peace? How has anger changed your path? How has anger caused you to waste time and energy? How have you sought out situations that would arouse anger in you? How have you or others been hurt by your anger? How have you suppressed your anger because you felt it wasn't acceptable or evolved? How have you dumped your anger on others?

Today let your relationship with anger be forever changed as you forgive yourself for it.

~ Now Meditate ~

# INTENTION
## for the day

## ☀ MORNING *writing*

## ☾ EVENING *reflections & gratitude*

# 50. MY Brothers AND Sisters ARE WORTHY OF MY forgiveness

Sometimes it's difficult to forgive because we see others as unworthy of being forgiven. We see them as unforgivable, needing permanent, everlasting punishment.

Does your condemnation accomplish anything? Does it stand to have any constructive effect whatsoever? If not, you must see that your condemnation is a waste of energy that corrupts your peace of mind. But that may not be enough to convince you that your brothers and sisters are worthy of your forgiveness.

So let's consider what worthy means – we mean possessing an innate worth just like you do, indistinguishable from yours, having the same heart, the same core awareness which is simply being expressed through a different body. When you deem your brothers and sisters worthy, you affirm your own worth. They are inseparable.

Your brothers and sisters are worthy not just of your forgiveness but of your Love. To love Spirit is to love the expressions of Spirit (your fellow humans, for instance). You don't have to start with the most difficult ones; love those who are easy to love, but do it more consciously. Then stretch a little. As Love moves through you with greater ease and your capacity increases, you can begin to love even those challenging cases.

Look into their eyes. Put down your weapons. Set aside your shield. Just be with them and you'll know.

*Now Meditate*

# INTENTION
## for the day

_____
_____
_____

## ☀ MORNING *writing*

_____
_____
_____
_____
_____
_____
_____
_____
_____

## ☾ EVENING *reflections & gratitude*

_____
_____
_____
_____
_____
_____
_____
_____

# 51.

# I *forgive* MYSELF
# FOR MY *Sadness*

The pain of sadness (in all its forms, including grief, despair, and depression) is only compounded when you disapprove of yourself for having it. When you focus on the disparity between how you are feeling and how you believe you *should* be feeling, you conclude, "Something is wrong with me." Besides magnifying your pain, treating yourself this way obstructs the potential for healing.

Sadness tends to congeal in us, dampening our ability to move and expand our consciousness, and perhaps, eventually crystalizing as physical impediments in our bodies. Our intention is not to spur fear or self-blame, but to awaken you to the necessity of healing. Sadness as a transient emotion is not harmful. Only when it is resisted and condemned is it condensed into a chronic and toxic pattern. Forgive and end this now.

When you feel sadness, don't run from it. See if you can meet it without judgment. When you feel sadness, what do you make it mean about you? Ask the sadness, "What are you?" Can you be curious? See if you can feel it without contracting. And forgive yourself, over and over.

Our hope for you is not the total absence of unpleasant emotions; it's the ability to experience them with an open heart, within a broader context of Love, and to release them. Love cushions the impact of these feelings and supports you to feel capable of managing them – and any circumstances they relate to. The love in your heart illuminates the story that gave rise to these emotions and reveals the freedom that's available to you.

## ～ *Now Meditate* ～

# INTENTION
### for the day

## ☀ MORNING *writing*

## ☾ EVENING *reflections & gratitude*

# 52. I AM *worthy* OF MY *love*

Like self-worth, your worthiness of love is an unchangeable fact. It's not up to your limited mind (or anyone else's) to decide. You were created by Love as Love. You *are* worthy of your Love. You're mistaken if you believe otherwise.

Often we treat Love as a gift that can be offered or withheld based on our moment-to-moment approval – like choosing to share or not share an ice cream cone. Relating to Love this way reinforces a gross misunderstanding of what it is and how it works. Love is beyond the petty manipulation of human personalities.

There is nothing you have done, said, or thought, nothing about how you look or feel that makes you unworthy of Love. It's uncomfortable to reckon with the ways in which you differ from the model human you've been taught to be. There are facets of you - and everyone - that are ugly and socially unacceptable. But withholding Love as a punishment just keeps you fragmented and deprived. Shining unlimited Love upon all of yourself can only make you stronger and healthier. And it offers you the profound peace of being undivided and totally honest, with nothing to hide.

If there are parts of yourself that you resist or deny or despise, let Love rush into them. They threaten to come out involuntarily only because you've tried to squeeze them into oblivion. Denying them Love won't help you discern their nature or determine what you need. Let your Love welcome and integrate them into an ever-expanding sense of your whole Self.

Open your heart to yourself and bask in your own Love.

*Now Meditate*

# INTENTION
## *for the day*

---

☀ MORNING *writing*

---

☾ EVENING *reflections & gratitude*

# 53.
# I *forgive* MYSELF FOR MY *fear*

Consider the ways you have experienced fear. How has it affected your life? What have you avoided doing because of fear? What communications have you been too afraid to make? What possibilities have you vetoed? How has your ability to enjoy life been compromised by it?

Fear is so primal, so deeply wired into your body to ensure its survival. When it blares through your system, it's so jarringly unpleasant – and perhaps associated with scary circumstances – that it leaves a deep imprint in your neurology and emotional body. The mind is keen to avoid such situations in the future, so it aggressively seeks to identify similar conditions and may go overboard at sounding the alarm.

## CONSCIOUSLY OPEN YOUR HEART

Ask to be reconfigured today. Ask to have your fear circuitry cleaned up and hauled away. Offer your fear to your Highest Self and ask to have it replaced with peace. When fear arises, don't resist it. Consciously open your heart. Keep breathing, deeply into the bowl of your pelvis. And forgive yourself again. You are stronger than you think.

*~ Now Meditate ~*

# INTENTION
## for the day

☀ MORNING *writing*

☾ EVENING *reflections & gratitude*

# 54.

## THERE IS NOTHING TO *fear*

Fear is a disconcerting frequency of energy that demands your attention when it moves through you, contracting your consciousness around a single priority: protection. The combination of fear and resistance creates a strong impression on your nervous system and emotional body that makes you prone to being retriggered, even when there is no real threat.

Of the many things you might fear – death, bodily harm, pain, embarrassment, loss – some may be possible, some potentially unpleasant, but nearly always the danger resides solely in your mind. *In this moment*, what is there to fear? Even "real" threats diminish in significance when seen in perspective. What you *really* are is so much more than this body. What you *really* are is beyond harm, and what you *really* have is beyond loss.

You chose this life; you chose to experience humanity knowing that you had the faculties to manage it, to *remember,* even in the face of great fear, that you are the Divine Light itself. Knowing that all of it – the triumph and suffering, the horror and awe – is part of your play, and that when you are eventually reabsorbed into the Whole of yourself, you will be supremely grateful.

As you practice inviting space into your everyday awareness, expanding into the You beyond this body and personality, feelings of fear are more like the momentary thrill of walking through a haunted house. You *know* you will emerge.

In the presence of fear, *remember:* You're not just a scared human, you're a Conscious Being who is *aware* of the scared human part of you. Don't resist the feeling. Breathe down into your pelvis, filling the bowl with your breath. Make your exhale long, letting go. Forgive yourself for feeling this. Stand up or sit tall, put your feet on the floor, and arouse your Love Warrior. Cut through this fear and embrace it with the full power of your heart.

*∽ Now Meditate ∽*

# INTENTION
## for the day

☀ MORNING *writing*

☾ EVENING *reflections & gratitude*

## 55. I BRING MY *consciousness* TO MY BREATH *throughout* EACH DAY

Besides bringing oxygen into your body, your breath serves numerous other useful functions. It calms your mind and helps you release stress. The mind follows the breath. Thus, as you slow and deepen your breathing, you settle and anchor your mind. Meanwhile, each exhale becomes more than a release of carbon dioxide, but an opportunity to let go.

Your breath takes away pain. It promotes movement where there is stagnation and discomfort. It connects you with the universe, each breath exchanging your atoms with those of the world, and the opening and closing of your body synchronizing you with the breath of Spirit.

It keeps you in the present. The breath is always now; putting your attention on it unites you with this moment.

Finally, it's a perpetual expression of the Name of God. With the delicate sound of every breath we speak that Name. Forget "God" and "Spirit" and "Divine" for now. Quiet your mind and listen to the coming and going of the breath of life within you.

It has been said that the word creates our world. And what comes before every word? Breath.

*Now Meditate*

# INTENTION
### for the day

## ☀ MORNING writing

## ☾ EVENING reflections & gratitude

## 56.

# I forgive myself

## FOR ANY TIME I HAVEN'T TREATED MYSELF WITH

# love AND kindness

The act of forgiveness often has multiple layers. For whenever we've condemned, there is the *condemner* (who must be forgiven), there is the act of *condemning* (which must be forgiven), and there is the one who has been *condemned* (who must be forgiven).

As you've aimed to do everything right, to get approval, and to succeed, there have been instances when you have attacked yourself for the mistakes you've made. But while you may have forgiven yourself for making mistakes (the condemned), you may not have addressed the self-blame that originated in response to having witnessed yourself being the condemner and doing the condemning. Now it's time to forgive those layers of blame. If you can't find this blame, but your experience is not predominantly one of ease and joy, look deeper.

If you haven't treated yourself with love and kindness, you only compound the damage by condemning yourself for it and withholding forgiveness. Say, "I forgive myself for attacking myself." Love yourself. Set yourself free.

## ∽ Now Meditate ∽

# INTENTION
## for the day

---

☀ MORNING *writing*

---
---
---
---
---
---
---

☾ EVENING *reflections & gratitude*

---
---
---
---
---
---
---

# 57. MY *Spirit* IS UNBREAKABLE

Your mind may be confused, your body may be in pain, and you may feel unhappy, but your Spirit is unbreakable. Un-sick-able. Undying. Unchanging. It is wholly unaffected by your circumstances. It loves and accepts you completely. It will always tell you the truth. And it will never leave you.

## YOU ARE ETERNAL SPIRIT

Not only are you *not broken* at this fundamental level, you are unbreakable. Beyond harm. And this is what you really are. It's that sense of You that has always been there, watching your life without judgement. Watching your mind and personality develop, watching your body grow and change, watching you do your best to get your needs met with the available resources. Throughout the years, it has always been there, always the same.

It's *so* familiar, *so* ever-present that you usually don't notice it. Like the air around you. Yet, if your mind and body were swept away, this would be what's left. Absolute consciousness. And you would likely exclaim, "Oh, *THIS! I AM* this!" While everything else in your life is constantly changing, this is the only *always*. You can invite this recognition into every moment, allowing it to shrink your problems. You are eternal Spirit, and you can't be broken.

*Now Meditate*

# INTENTION
### for the day

## ☀ MORNING *writing*

## ☾ EVENING *reflections & gratitude*

# 58. IT IS SAFE FOR ME TO
## *play*
## IN THIS
## LIFE

There is no reason not to play. Perhaps you find yourself being very serious about life. You tell yourself there is important work to do, there is danger, people are suffering. Yes, these are part of the world. But denying your basic nature, allowing gratitude and fascination to be overridden by seriousness, won't make you more respectful or effective.

You *do* have important work here. Devoting yourself to it with happiness in your heart and turning it into a conscious play will make you more effective. Your work is part of your play. Not only is it safe for you to play, but the more you give yourself over to it, the closer you will come to living the life your soul chose. You will be freer, more powerful, more at ease, more creative, more intuitive, and more present when you embrace *play*.

## TO BE CAREFREE IS AUTHENTICALLY YOU

God doesn't want you to restrict yourself from playing. You chose this play, emerging as the world for the pure delight of it. You can either follow through on that choice or pretend you didn't choose it – that your Highest Self would want you to feel serious and burdened instead. You *did* choose it. Remember. To be carefree is authentically You; it fosters healing in yourself and others; it corrects generations of guilt, shame, and self-punishment. So, choose what you've already chosen. Play!

*Now Meditate*

# INTENTION
## for the day

## ☀ MORNING *writing*

## ☾ EVENING *reflections & gratitude*

# 59. I FORGIVE MYSELF FOR

## Attacking

## THE WORLD

When you look upon the world do you see perfection? Or are there parts you simply cannot accept? For all the ways in which the world is not how you believe it should be, you have attacked it. For all the "evil" you perceive in the world, you have attacked it. All the people you see as immoral or wrong, you have attacked them. The billboards you dislike. The laws. The garbage. The smell. The weather. The insurance. The politics.

It's likely you also blame the world for ways in which you feel dissatisfied – for cutting you off from God, for not loving you unconditionally, for not providing you with as much money as you'd like, for offering so many temptations that are bad for you, for not completely approving of you, for being confusing, for making it hard for you.

There are the parts of the world you admire and accept and parts that you look upon with disapproval. Although it may not be readily perceptible to you, you've witnessed your attacks on the world, you've recorded the times you haven't treated others with kindness, and there is a certain burden of guilt and shame for this. You probably have even felt hurt from the understanding that you're inseparable from this world you attack. All of this may be imperceptible, so go deep in your meditation with determination to root out these poisonous thoughts.

Forgive yourself today for this attack. Forgive the whole complex of this condemnation: the attacker (you), the act of attacking (violence, resistance, and judgment), and the attacked (the world and everything about it you don't accept). When you endeavor to find true peace, you must forgive everything. There are layers upon layers of blame, and at the juicy center, freedom.

### Now Meditate

# INTENTION
## for the day

## ☀ MORNING *writing*

## ☾ EVENING *reflections & gratitude*

# 60.
# *All* attack *is* self-attack

Attacking others and the world, even if only in your mind, has a powerful impact on you. First, it reinforces the belief that you are fundamentally separate and different from them. When you say to yourself that a certain person or group is bad, or that a place is ugly, or that a situation is wrong, you assert your isolation from it.

Second, you restrict your freedom. As you condemn particular elements of the world, you ensure that similar traits in yourself can never be safely acknowledged. This means you can't be all of who you are, nor can you reconcile your inner conflict.

Third, it generates a subconscious fear of retaliation. Because, if the world knew how viciously you attack it, wouldn't it attack you back?

Thus, these criticisms produce guilt. They corrupt your peace of mind. They make the world unsafe. And they hinder your awakening to an inclusive *unity consciousness*.

Today, pay special attention to the ways you criticize the world. Notice how you seek to control and restrict the world. See if you can feel the way each criticism destabilizes you and makes you feel less at ease. Then, choose something different.

*Now Meditate*

# INTENTION
## for the day

## ☼ MORNING *writing*

## ☾ EVENING *reflections & gratitude*

# 61. MY *purpose* TODAY IS TO *forgive the world*

Even if you don't feel like you're actively fighting with the world, you have your gripes. Perhaps they're greater in number than you think. How many ways do you believe the world should be different than it is? How many things in the world do you see as wrong?

The world is held within your consciousness; you might be dreaming the whole thing. But regardless of the condition or existence of an objective world, the world that lives in your mind dominates your attention. And as long as you condemn it, your condemnation and the object of this condemnation all reside within you. *You* are the unforgiven.

## IT'S PERFECT JUST AS IT IS

Imagine the relief you could experience if you let all of this go. What if it were no longer your responsibility to keep tabs on the world, to take positions on it, to pass judgment, or to fix it? What if you *knew* – really, truly, without a doubt – that it's perfect just as it is? How will you feel when you're no longer holding the world hostage in your mind, withholding acceptance until it meets your secret conditions? This state is available to you. You need only to forgive.

No grudges. No regrets. Nothing resisted. Let the world be. Set it free. Tell yourself, "My purpose today is to forgive everything and everyone in the world."

*Now Meditate*

# INTENTION
## for the day

_____

## ☀ MORNING _writing_

_____
_____
_____
_____
_____

## ☾ EVENING _reflections & gratitude_

_____
_____
_____
_____
_____
_____

62.

# I release the world from my CONTROL

The desire to exert control over your life reinforces the belief that you lack control. How do you feel when you believe that the world needs to be controlled by you in order for things to turn out well? And how do you feel when you believe you lack control over your life or the world? Is it inevitable that if you can't be in control, things won't turn out well?

When you aim to control the world, even if only in your mind, clenching with your will around a situation you are concerned about, you only contract your own consciousness and freedom.

## THANK GOODNESS THIS IS ALL BEING TAKEN CARE OF

How would you feel if you believed that the future was out of your hands, but that it was *all being taken care of* in a way that would serve your highest good? What if you could put your future in the hands of Spirit and completely relax in that? What if you could put the future in the hands of your Highest Self and never worry about it again? Today, let your mantra be "Thank goodness this is all being taken care of."

*Now Meditate*

# INTENTION
*for the day*

## ☀ MORNING *writing*

## ☾ EVENING *reflections & gratitude*

# 63.

## what i forgive in one benefits all

We are all connected, collectively perpetuating the same illusions and collectively craving love and forgiveness. We even share most of the same deep beliefs, through what Carl Jung called the "collective unconscious." And one of the most prevalent and damaging of these beliefs is that we all have reason to be guilty. Whether it's because Eve ate the apple, or because we cut ourselves off from God, or we hurt our parents, or some other long-forgotten crime, there's *something* we must have done that we'll eventually have to pay for.

We rarely give our conscious consent to adopting this guilt, and a lifetime often passes without ever questioning it. It is reinforced by every mind that perpetuates it, and it appears to be validated by every human crime.

But it is dissolved by every act of forgiveness.

No change occurs in isolation from the whole. When you really, truly forgive, release from the burden of guilt spreads like dividing cells. The one forgiven becomes two, because you receive whatever you give. Then this liberation ripples throughout our shared consciousness, challenging the correctness of this guilt, loosening its hold on us, terminating generations of guilty echoes.

Forgive today, knowing you open countless cages.

## Now Meditate

# INTENTION
## for the day

## ☀ MORNING *writing*

## ☾ EVENING *reflections & gratitude*

# 64.

## THE *other person* IS *me*

Every person is you. The person you hate. The person you envy. The person you admire. The person you love. There is no quality any person possesses that is not also within you. As long as you can point at another person, and say, "We have nothing in common," – you don't truly know yourself.

## THE DIVINE IS IN EVERYONE'S EYES

Your disdain for another is an opportunity to recognize your disdain for yourself – and heal it. Your admiration for another is an opportunity to recognize their merits in yourself – and to love and approve of yourself. Your hatred of another is an opportunity to recognize the aspects of your own shadow that you won't accept – and accept and forgive them.

Apply this today to everyone you interact with. The Divine is in everyone's eyes. Look into them and see yourself.

*Now Meditate*

# INTENTION
## for the day

☀ MORNING *writing*

☾ EVENING *reflections & gratitude*

# 65. I AM *one* WITH THE *divine*

All that is, is God. Everything is One. There is no *other*. And in this reality, one plus one equals one.

Only by dividing One can it become two. And such division happens exclusively within the limited perception of the mind. It's a nearly unavoidable product of how the mind works. It relies on labels and categories – on organizing things by how they *differ* from each other. It's a valuable tool for operating as a human being, but it's simply incapable of truly grasping the unity in all things. That's the dominion of the vast consciousness you usually ignore – in favor of the illusion of safety and control you identify with your mind, body, and possessions.

A single glimpse of reality would convince you that your oneness with the Divine is the most obvious truth. You are the Oneness. You are of the Oneness. You are entirely contained within Oneness. And because Oneness encompasses everything, there is nothing else. Oneness is Love, Awareness, Peace. And it is eternal.

What does this mean for you? It means different things to different facets of you. To the scared part of you, it means no harm will ever come to what you really are. To the lonely part of you, it means you are never alone. To the fragmented part of yourself, it means you are whole. To the sick part of you, it means nothing is wrong. And to the you that is ready to wake up, it means the person with these "parts" is already One with the Source itself.

*Now Meditate*

# INTENTION
## for the day

☀ MORNING *writing*

☾ EVENING *reflections & gratitude*

# 66. I forgive EVERYONE WHO HAS EVER CAUSED ME pain OR harm

If you want more complete joy, greater freedom, and deeper peace, you will eventually need to look at who you aren't forgiving.

Consider the possibility that lifelong punishment may be cruel and unusual. You might ask yourself, "How long will I hold onto this before it will be enough?" or, "How much longer am I going to pollute myself with this grievance?" Poison yourself no longer with this resentment.

Where *in your present reality* are these evil deeds of the past? They live now only in your mind. If there is no action today that can be taken to fix what has been done, what is there to do but forgive?

Don't do it if you believe you're being magnanimous by pardoning them – because they don't really deserve it, but you're going to take the high road. Such an attitude just magnifies the sense of separation between you and the other party and reinforces their guilt.

You'll know it's true forgiveness when you don't wish for them to suffer any longer, when you don't want them to continue to feel guilt, and when you want them to experience peace – just as you want peace for yourself. This is a step toward union. Every act of forgiveness brings nearer the restoration of your native state of peace, freedom, and joy.

*Now Meditate*

# INTENTION
## for the day

☀ MORNING *writing*

_____

☾ EVENING *reflections & gratitude*

# I CHOOSE *happiness*

All emotions are not created equal. Happiness isn't merely the positive equivalent of unhappiness. It's more than an emotion; it's your *native* state, the state that naturally emerges when you're in alignment with your Truth (Spirit). When you let go of your illusions and resentments, happiness is there – *uncaused*. The more you relinquish your condemnation of yourself and the world, the more easily your native state – happiness, peace, and innocence – is able to rise from your fundamental ground.

When you discover you are holding resentments, when you're focused on problems instead of blessings, when you're trying to control the world, or you've given the driver's seat to your thoughts and feelings, it's time to remember your power of choice. What do you choose today – ego or Spirit? Arrogance or humility? Illusion or freedom? Do you want to be *right* about your misesrable point of view or *happy*?

This must be an active choice. If you adopt your perspective passively or unconsciously, cultural influences and habitual wiring may persuade you to default to dissatisfaction. Your ego has told you that only it can procure the conditions that will make you happy. Choosing happiness from your very core will wake you up from this spell. This choice provides an energy that will guide your thoughts and actions, and it makes you more effective at serving the world.

Don't deny or resist negative emotions. By all means, identify what you're actually feeling and accept it. Let discomfort reveal your limiting beliefs and untrue thoughts. Use it to show you what needs to be let go, cleaned up, or healed. Meanwhile, remember that it need not eclipse the Truth. Align yourself with what is for your highest good and the highest good of the world. Choose happiness.

*Now Meditate*

# INTENTION
## for the day

☀ MORNING *writing*

☽ EVENING *reflections & gratitude*

# 68.
# Creation cannot be complete without receiving

Any way in which you might wish to shape your life is an expression of change. And change is a product of two main energies: creativity and receptivity. Creativity is choosing an intention and expressing it, like planting a seed. Receptivity is the ability to be responsive and adaptive – to receive that seed and support it. Both need to be present in order for you to effectively shape your world in a purposeful way. You have probably consciously practiced the former more than the latter.

We're not suggesting that you need to actively change your world in order to be at peace. In fact, our hope is that you experience peace regardless of the current state of your life. But you may at times feel moved to play a more active role in initiating change, and then an understanding of this dynamic may serve you. Some reasons for choosing to more actively shape your life might include: for the play of it, to be of service, to experience something different, to share healing and Love, to express a purpose, or to create beauty.

Lasting change requires a welcoming and a willingness for the creative impulse to take form in you and your world. You may sometimes experience it like being the follower in a couples dance, where your role is to *yield* to the lead without losing the form.

As you endeavor to manifest anything in your life, see if you can equally play with these two energies of creativity and receptivity.

*Now Meditate*

# INTENTION
*for the day*

## ☀ MORNING *writing*

## ☾ EVENING *reflections & gratitude*

# 69.

# I *open* MYSELF TO *receiving*

Receptivity is an opening.

It can feel like holding open a space in yourself. It may even feel a little like stretching. It takes some discipline to keep this space from filling up with old patterns and thoughts (your ego is likely to present some compelling ones) or tightening up because the change feels uncomfortable and different. It's more apt to happen when you feel desperate, when you believe that you really, *really* need something. These reflexive forms of *closing* make it hard to receive. It's like extending a clenched fist to accept the gift God is holding out for you. Stay open and soft. You'll get what you need.

When you act to initiate change, ensure that you make space in yourself and your life to receive something new, and that there is also space in your *self-image* to allow for an updated version of you. It can sometimes be a challenge to form a new image of your life and fully accept this image. If you're unable to receive the revision when it arrives, you may find yourself reverting to former ways.

If change doesn't come, or comes but doesn't last, it's possible that the creative intention wasn't clear or that it was driven by fear rather than Love. But it's just as likely that you're simply not *receiving* it.

Be an open vessel. Your mantra for today is *Open*. Repeat liberally and with feeling.

*Now Meditate*

# INTENTION
## for the day

☀ MORNING *writing*

☾ EVENING *reflections & gratitude*

# 70.

# *Who would I be if I had no resistance?*

Today's lesson lies entirely in what you can learn from asking yourself a single question and being willing to hear the answer. Ask yourself as often as you think of it – especially when you feel uncomfortable, bored, upset, critical, disappointed, impatient, unhappy, tired, blocked, or anything other than peaceful.

## GO DEEP

We encourage you to direct the question not just to your mind, but also your body, your soul, and your Highest Self. There is no additional explanation to offer; let the question go deep within you and receive the guidance that comes.

*Now Meditate*

# INTENTION
## for the day

☀ MORNING *writing*

☾ EVENING *reflections & gratitude*

# 71

# I *am* IMPERTURBABLE

When someone shatters a wine glass with their voice, they are taking advantage of the phenomenon of resonance. The glass has a certain resonant frequency – that is, the particular pitch at which sound waves cause the glass to vibrate. If the sound is loud enough, these waves will move the glass so dramatically that it breaks. In order for you to be perturbed by the world, you must resonate with whatever ideas or behaviors perturb you.

A tone that's higher or lower than the glass's resonant frequency doesn't affect it. It's a similar case with being insulted by a person who speaks a language you don't understand. They could be saying the most hateful things, but their words pass through you harmlessly.

In actuality, the stuff that perturbs you is harmless anyway, in the big scheme of things. And it's okay if you get perturbed – forgive yourself and let it go. But the experience of imperturbability is a special one, and it awakens you to The Truth about yourself: that what you really are is eternal and can't be threatened.

Meditation is the single most powerful device for shifting your resonant frequency such that the world's drama no longer has the capacity to shatter you. With ongoing practice, you'll find that the things that would have been disturbing or tempting in the past just don't have the same ability to move you. You're no longer resonating at the "drama channel." What a relief.

Have you ever played the game of First One to Get Upset Loses? Why not try it today?

*Now Meditate*

# INTENTION
## for the day

☀ MORNING *writing*

☾ EVENING *reflections & gratitude*

# 72.

## As I speak of others I speak of myself

When you hear yourself speaking about someone, pay attention. The way you hold them reveals how you hold yourself. If you truly respect and love yourself, you don't diminish others.

The negative things you say about others are a valuable indication of where your relationship with yourself needs healing. The qualities you scorn in others show you what you're unable to tolerate in yourself – and thus, where your freedom is limited by your shadow aspect. The shadow portion of your personality includes everything you deny possessing, everything you hide from the world and yourself, everything about yourself you're afraid to come to terms with. Yet, you may be vigilant to discover these qualities in others and even to point them out. Notice this. There's something here for you.

In contrast, when you lift others up with your words, you are yourself elevated. The recognition of virtue awakens your own virtue. When you speak to this you dissolve the illusion of separation between yourself and another. You are united. Your kind words invite Love into the world.

When you see the Light in another, name it. Proclaim it. You speak of yourself.

## Now Meditate

# INTENTION
## for the day

☀ MORNING *writing*

🌙 EVENING *reflections & gratitude*

# 73.

## I honor the power of my words

Even if you feel you're not the kind of person who relies on others, even if you claim to expect nothing from the world, even if you have no faith in anything, you still hope, perhaps secretly, that someone will someday make things better.

That someday is today. That someone is you.

The hero of your story has been here all along.

Because you weren't aware of this, you've treated your word frivolously. At times, perhaps it's been little more than a means of complaining and getting people's approval. You didn't take your agreements seriously because you didn't understand their full implications and power.

Our intention is not to scold you, but to correct a misunderstanding. Word, in its purest form, is the Divine itself. It constitutes the structure of reality. It unifies ideation and manifestation, your inner world and outer world. It is the means by which you take a conscious role in shaping life.

Choose to hear the sacred sound of the true words that arise within you and emanate into the world. Choose to honor the power of your words from this day forward and let your actions be congruent with them.

*Now Meditate*

# INTENTION
## for the day

---

☀ MORNING *writing*

---

☾ EVENING *reflections & gratitude*

# 74. LESS *resistance* MEANS GREATER *ease* AND *energy*

One of the basic principles of traditional martial arts is that a good fighter is able to stay relaxed while simultaneously directing their power at the challenge at hand. This applies to life as a whole – you'll be most effective when you're able to stay *relaxed* even while directing your power into a demanding task.

As you learn to maintain a more constant awareness of what's happening in your body, always keeping a portion of your attention on how you feel, you'll recognize the presence of resistance, and you'll be able to let it go more quickly and easily.

And each time you do this you'll notice a lightening of your body and spirit, and an experience of greater ease. Each act of letting go may cause only a subtle shift, but as this becomes a habitual practice – to continuously shed resistance – the change in your energy will become increasingly significant.

You'll notice when you're resisting that you're usually not trusting. When you trust, your experience becomes spacious rather than contracted, and ease and energy naturally flow through you.

*Now Meditate*

# INTENTION
## for the day

☀ MORNING *writing*

☾ EVENING *reflections & gratitude*

# 75.

# When I release my RESENTMENT, I see a world of magic

The world is a magical place. You knew it once. Perhaps you've forgotten or even scorned the idea. But the magic hasn't disappeared, it's just hidden.

Most of us see our relationship with the world as one of mutual manipulation. The world delivers circumstances seemingly at random, and it's difficult not to take them personally. A blessing today – "Oh, thank you! I must be doing something right!" A tragedy tomorrow – "Why me? What did I do to deserve this?" Our only hope seems to be finding a way to hack the system or becoming so disengaged that we're unaffected by the ups and downs. It's a sadly unmagical existence.

If you're like everyone else, you carry some resentment toward the world for this. You resent it for not playing by a fixed set of rules – or for never sharing those rules with you. You've done your part – you went to school, you worked your ass off, you tried to be a good person, yet the world hasn't delivered as expected.

Meanwhile, magic is always happening, but you're tuned to a different station. Diligently releasing your resentment opens you to a new plane of experience. There's so much magic – phenomena and connections that have no scientific explanation – that your mind will quickly attempt to find another channel of disbelief to obscure your vision. Stay open. Pay attention. This is just the beginning.

~ *Now Meditate* ~

# INTENTION
## for the day

☼ MORNING *writing*

☾ EVENING *reflections & gratitude*

# 76.
# *Nature* IS ALWAYS *teaching,* *aligning,* AND *guiding*

Nature is the perfect teacher, guide, and calibrator. Let the intelligence that created you teach you about yourself and bring you back to balance. If you approach Nature as a student, you will be taught in the ways of cosmic order and humanity.

Spend quality time with Nature. Don't regard it as mere scenery. Invite it into your life. Go outdoors. Integrate objects of Nature into your living and working spaces. Forge a routine that is connected to the natural world and its cycles. Pay attention and you'll notice how the substances and dynamics of Nature are reflected in your own life. When you encounter a challenge, imagine how the dynamic might be expressed in the natural world and meditate on how Nature would resolve this harmoniously.

Winter is a time of stillness and potential, of dormancy and stored resources. It's a good time for rest and regeneration. It's the seed phase. Spring is the oomph of breaking out of winter's crust and launching new plans. It's a time of growth, structure, and vision. It's the seedling phase. Summer brings the zenith of this growth and a great communion of intermingling creatures of all kinds. It's boisterous and beautiful. It's the flowering phase. Late summer, the fruiting phase, has a distinctly different energy, with grains and produce ripening for harvest. It's a time of abundance and nourishment, of reaping the benefits of what has been sown. Autumn signals a downturn in energy, a phase of decline. Plants wither and leaves fall. The sun drops to a lower arc in the sky. It's a time for letting go and reflecting on the inner essence of things. Then it's winter again.

This is the rhythm of your life – in each endeavor, and in your existence as a whole. But don't take our word for it. Put your bare skin on the ground and learn directly from the master.

## ～ *Now Meditate* ～

# INTENTION
## for the day

☀ MORNING *writing*

☾ EVENING *reflections & gratitude*

# 77. MY *flexibility*

## ALLOWS ME TO RESPOND WITH

### *grace*

## TO WHAT *life* BRINGS

Like humans, trees span the realm between earth and sky. Like every tree you are rooted in the earth. You're grounded in the material world and your sense of self is oriented around the body you occupy. And like every tree, you grow upward, striving toward something transcendent and unseen. You grow from potential to expression, from a seed to a mighty tree. And like any healthy tree, you are served on this journey by the quality of flexibility.

Flexibility is the opposite of rigidity, the opposite of a fixed, static, immovable viewpoint. It entails meeting life organically, based on how it really is, rather than on your stories or beliefs. It asks you to let go of the need to be right. Rather than throwing the pieces on the floor when you encounter an obstacle, flexibility keeps you in the game. Like a supple vine, you find a healthy way to grow around it.

When you encounter something unexpected, which is most definitely to be expected, with flexibility you meet it openly; you dance with it; you learn something new. Flexibility is unattached to the specifics of how the will of your Highest Self is expressed through you. Knowing you will be an emissary of Love, flexibility says, "Use me. I don't need to be in control. I don't need to dictate the terms."

Today, challenge yourself to be more flexible of both body and mind.

## ∽ *Now Meditate* ∽

# INTENTION
## for the day

☀ MORNING *writing*

☾ EVENING *reflections & gratitude*

# 78. I CHOOSE TO PUT MY *attention* ON THE *blessing* IN MY LIFE

Your attention is drawn to your problems, like your tongue to a sore in your mouth, unable to stop visiting it. It's natural for problems to get more of your attention than the things that are working in your life, because real problems need fixing. If there were a leak in your boat, it would be wise to pay more attention to the hole than to the functional parts of the boat.

Such allocation of attention works when you're accurate about identifying actual problems and your goal is to resolve them. But when your attention is given away to problems without any intention of resolution or letting go; when you find yourself *searching* for problems; when you're occupied with *potential* problems and other people's problems; when you *generate* problems through a wide array of critical observations about yourself and the world, you are effectively spoiling your life.

This habit makes the focus of your life the parts you *don't* like rather than the parts you *do* like. It narrows your awareness to your mind's illusions rather than opening it to the truth. And it *is* simply a habit.

Be disciplined about how you use your attention. Catch yourself indulging in problem-spotting and criticism, and put your attention on *anything* else. Meanwhile, make a new habit of noticing what is working well in your life. Every day, recognize, be grateful for, share, proclaim, and amplify the *blessings*. In this way, you'll not only tremendously improve your experience of life, you'll also naturally invite more blessings to appear.

*∽ Now Meditate ∽*

# INTENTION
## for the day

☀ MORNING *writing*

☾ EVENING *reflections & gratitude*

# 79.

## RECOGNIZING MY *worth* EMPOWERS OTHERS TO DO THE *same*

Your self-worth is an unchanging fact, regardless of your awareness of it. When you do start to become aware of it, you embody it in a way that's perceptible to others. Even if they're not conscious of it, they see an inkling of your light, your love, your vastness – your *worth* – and it calls to their own worth, inviting it to emerge.

## WATCH THE WORLD TAKE FLIGHT

While you may have experienced feeling inferior or jealous of others who consciously embody their worth, and while you may have sympathy for those who are struggling, don't allow yourself to suppress it for the sake of not making others feel bad. The greatest gift you can give the world is recognize and become what you really are.

You're not responsible for how others' minds may distort what they see in you. When you consciously embody your worth, you show them what they're capable of. Even if they're unable to embrace it in this moment, it jogs a deep recognition, like holding up a mirror that reveals their long-forgotten wings.

Fly. And watch the world take flight.

*Now Meditate*

# INTENTION
## for the day

## ☀ MORNING *writing*

## ☾ EVENING *reflections & gratitude*

# 80. NOTHING OF *True value* IS EVER *lost*

All human cycles mirror the cycles of the seasons. In winter, life awaits in dormant roots and snow-covered seeds. It's a time of stillness and potential. Spring brings an awakening of new life and new plans. It's a time of hope and determination. Summer is about expansive growth, blossoming, and fruiting. It's a time of joyful connection and abundance. Finally, in the aptly named *fall*, energy declines and retreats inward. Flowers close and shrivel, leaves die and drop, and trees stand bare.

If we perceive this phase as a loss – if we cling to material elements of what we've been through – it's a time of nostalgia and grief. But if we recognize that nothing of true value can be lost, then it's a time of crystal clear reflection. When nothing stands in the way, we can see *precisely* and *brilliantly* the everlasting gift in the experience. Growth can't be lost.

In anything you might seek to protect from loss – your body, your possessions, your personality, your family – the value is in your relationship with that person or thing, in the Love, the healing, and the connection it brings you. The absence of the physical expression of that relationship doesn't negate the relationship or its value. The worth of these protected things is in experiencing and uniting with their essence – and coming back to yourself, more whole than ever.

Love, experience, consciousness, play, growth, and connection – these greatest treasures of our lives are un-lose-able.

*Now Meditate*

# INTENTION
## for the day

☀ MORNING *writing*

☾ EVENING *reflections & gratitude*

# 81. I *feel* AND *release*
## MY
## RESISTANCE
## TO
## DEATH

The gift of life is like God handing you a sparkler. You could dance with it, make beautiful patterns, marvel at the way it lights up the night, share it with others, and savor every awesome second. Or you could stand there frozen, crying, "Oh no, it's going to burn out! Oh no, it's going to burn out! Oh no, it's going to burn out!" until it finally does.

Don't let the fear of death spoil your experience of the gift of life. Today, bring to mind the idea of your death. Like everyone who has ever walked the planet, your body will die. It is the most inevitable, natural thing. What is it about your death that you find most objectionable? The prospect of experiencing pain? Being afraid before it happens? Leaving behind sad loved ones? Losing this human life?

Close your eyes and bring one of these objectionable ideas to mind. As you hold it in your consciousness, notice how your body responds. Feel the resistance. Perhaps there's a tightness, a jitteriness, or some other sensation. Where is it? Can you be curious about it? Can you experience it willingly? See if you can allow it to open and spread, inviting it to be felt and experienced completely. Breathe into it and let it go. Repeat this process with the same idea (if it still feels strong) or another concern about death. Can you relinquish the fight and make peace with it? Can you be open to the possibility that death is not what you think it is?

*~ Now Meditate ~*

# INTENTION
## for the day

☀ MORNING *writing*

☾ EVENING *reflections & gratitude*

# 82. I *choose* TO LIVE IN MY *present* EXPERIENCE

One of the most insidious tendencies of the mind is to remove us from the present. Often we are revisiting the past, feeling nostalgic or regretful, or just watching old stories. Other times, we're anticipating the future, worrying about unpleasant possibilities, fantasizing about finally getting to the state we've been chasing for so many years. Or we're just somewhere else, immersed in thoughts that have nothing to do with what we're currently engaged in.

The cost is higher than it seems. You're trading *real life* for mental illusions. There is a richness in the present experience that's lost as soon as you depart in your mind. Those moments of real presence are so rich – and rare – that they become the memories we revisit the most.

Today, we urge you to *choose* to live in your present experience rather than retreating into your mind. If you're experiencing anger, depression, or some other form of pain, ask yourself, "*In this moment* what's the problem?" And if you find you've gone into the past or future or some daydream, bring yourself back. Be with whatever you're engaged in. Let that be enough. If you're eating food, just eat food and notice that you're eating food. If you're driving your car, just drive your car and notice that you're driving the car. And if you're meditating, just sit, breathe, and notice that you're sitting and breathing. When you discover you've given your attention to your mind, simply take it back and give it to the present.

~ *Now Meditate* ~

# INTENTION
*for the day*

☀ MORNING *writing*

☾ EVENING *reflections & gratitude*

# 83. Every hardship is an opportunity to let go

What parts of life are hard for you? Take a look at your hardship today, and ask yourself these questions. First, *what's wrong with hard?* We understand that you may prefer easy, but is it possible to see hard as just hard, and not *wrong?* Like a workout should be. Like a day of farm work. Hard, but manageable.

Second, *what is my role in the perception of this situation as hard?* While there are certain circumstances that nearly anyone would perceive as *objectively* hard – like carrying boulders – others are only *subjectively* hard because of your personal viewpoint. Hardship is a state of mind that can be difficult to relinquish. Perhaps you were taught that hard work is noble, or that it's the only way to achieve anything, or that easy equals lazy. Such notions could lead you to believe you get extra credit for leading a *hard life.*

Third, *could I let go of my feelings about this situation?* Hold the situation in mind and feel what comes up in your body. Feel willingly. Invite the feeling. Welcome it. Breathe into it. And let it go.

Fourth, *what's possible when I let go?* What's beneath that hardship? When you view your hardship as an opportunity to let go, a tremendous array of additional opportunities arise. Thus, every hardship becomes an opportunity to wake up, to forgive, to practice changing perspective, to find new ways to play, to put what you've been learning to the test, to practice flexibility, to reunite with a fragmented part of yourself, to level up, to reaffirm your values, to practice going with the flow, to use your gifts, to connect with someone, to grow, to live your purpose, to relinquish control, to be supported, to choose lightness, to experience trust, to love yourself, and to become who you really are.

~ *Now Meditate* ~

# INTENTION
## for the day

☀ MORNING *writing*

☾ EVENING *reflections & gratitude*

# 84. EVERY ACT OF

## *letting go*

## BRINGS A GREATER

## *experience*

## OF

## *freedom*

It's probably easy for you understand why letting go of a negative emotion or a limiting thought will make you freer. But perhaps it's less obvious why your freedom expands also from the release of positive feelings or your attachment to things that give you pleasure.

Freedom is a condition of unattachment – whether to shackles or flowers. If you have a good experience, and you think, "I want it to always be this way," you are potentially as enslaved as if you think of a negative experience, "I want it to never be this way." That is, you are enslaved to the particular, narrow set of conditions that don't provoke resistance in you.

If this moment is a good one for you and you cling to it, like to trying to stop a film from moving to the next frame, you're denying what you *know* to be the truth – that life is dynamic and that clinging can only disconnect you from the present. The same is true when you revisit past moments and hope to settle an unresolved argument or dwell forever in an idyllic point in time. All such efforts are a departure from the reality of Now.

Every moment brings a new opportunity to let go, and as you do, this moment is immediately replaced by the next one. Letting go – even of the moments of bliss – is not loss. It can do nothing but bring you greater freedom, deeper peace, and alignment with the Great Truth.

## *Now Meditate*

# INTENTION
## for the day

☀ MORNING *writing*

☾ EVENING *reflections & gratitude*

# 85. ALL THINGS OF TRUE VALUE

*grow*

WHEN

*given*

If you give someone your sandwich, you won't have a sandwich anymore. But the kindness you offered – there's more of that now than there was before.

In the mind's world of duality, when something is given it's lost. But in reality, offerings of value amplify that value for both the giver and the receiver. By *true value,* we mean that which promotes greater alignment with or awareness of your Divine Nature – such as love, acceptance, peace, light, presence, truth, beauty, forgiveness, wisdom, and kindness. In truth, such an act of giving is more like God sharing God with God than it is a transfer of value.

If you want more of these qualities in your life, give them to others. When you make yourself a channel for such values, you are inevitably a recipient of the same. If you want forgiveness, offer forgiveness. If you want love, love others. If you want peace, offer peace. These can never be exhausted, and there is no end to the world's capacity to receive them or your capacity to give them.

*∽ Now Meditate ∽*

# INTENTION
## for the day

## ☀ MORNING *writing*

## ☾ EVENING *reflections & gratitude*

# 86. FORGIVENESS *opens* ME TO THE *truth*

Our resentments often play a significant role in shaping the script we live by, consuming our energy and attention, influencing our pursuits, perhaps even fueling the righteousness by which we justify sacrificing happiness and peace. But forgiveness is like peeling away the stories we overlaid upon the Truth. As you forgive and forgive, you remove veil after veil, and the undiluted Light that you are becomes increasingly bright.

## WHEN YOU FORGIVE, YOU STOP DICTATING THE TERMS

When you relinquish the desire to control how the world should be and how *you* should be, you and the world are released from your constraint. And in the space that opens up, you are able to recognize and be at peace with the Truth. In fact, you may experience it as a *remembering* of what you've always known . . . that all of creation is the play of the Divine.

When you forgive, you stop dictating the terms. Everything is allowed to be just as it is. And you feel unfathomably grateful to be a part of it.

*∼ Now Meditate ∼*

# INTENTION
## for the day

☀ MORNING *writing*

☾ EVENING *reflections & gratitude*

# 87. *There is no* SEPARATION

It is said that your physical eyes, being two, see only duality and separation, while your "third eye" – your higher consciousness – being one, sees only oneness and unity. Even though your two eyes show you many different things, all of them apparently separate, your inner sight sees the *oneness* that creates and unifies them all.

## SHOW ME MY ONENESS

To paraphrase Christopher Wallis's analogy, we are like seven billion mountain peaks poking up from a giant underwater continent. Because the water hides the bulk of these mountains, you perceive only a sliver of what you are, and everyone appears to be separate and disconnected from everyone else. But if you look below the surface, you'll see that we are all expressions of a singular Being.

There is no separation, and all of you – except the very tip of the mountain where your consciousness tends to reside – knows this and experiences it as *self-evident*. You are perfectly able to access this state of Unity Consciousness. Just meditate.

We can think of no way to say it more clearly, no reason to make it more complicated. You are one with everything. Sit in silence and make space in yourself. Sacrifice your thoughts for a little while, abstain from filling that space. And ask your Highest Self, "Show me my oneness. Help me experience this."

*Now Meditate*

# INTENTION
## for the day

※ MORNING *writing*

☾ EVENING *reflections & gratitude*

# 88. The *Awakening* of the world depends on my *Awakening*

The *whole world* can't awaken without you. It's not so much an obligation to participate – like everyone is in the car, honking the horn while you're sitting on the couch watching reality television. It's more like the world is waiting for you to start dancing so the party can begin.

Your role in the awakening of the world is a matter of making a *choice*, a choice that will resonate through innumerable minds. In fact, you are co-choosing this with countless others. As you lift out of your illusions, the world's eyelids crack open.

## THE WORLD IS WAITING FOR YOU TO START DANCING SO THE PARTY CAN BEGIN

Awakeness desires only awakeness. It seeks to wake up the still-sleeping parts of the universe. Like a bright-eyed child in the early morning, who wants the whole household to arise. Do you remember feeling that way? Clear away whatever sleepiness the years have piled on and *wake up*.

*Now Meditate*

# INTENTION
## for the day

## ☼ MORNING writing

## ☾ EVENING reflections & gratitude

## 89.

# Lightness is always available.

# I choose to be light

Light is used in everyday language to denote the quality of being *luminous* and also the quality of being *weightless*. We mean it both ways here. The ability to feel relatively weightless – as in unburdened, not heavy – and the quality of being a source of light, are made available to you at all times.

One of these qualities speaks to your human experience and the other more to your transcendent experience. For the physical you and the mind associated with it, accessing lightness allows you not to feel downtrodden by life; not to take it so seriously. To be truly lighthearted. For the transcendent you, the offering of lightness is to embody what you are – Love itself – to shine it so brightly within yourself as to leave nothing excluded, and to do so also in the world.

No circumstance can deprive you of this choice. Lightness wants to enter and illuminate the darkness, like a sea of Love pressing up against a closed door.

Open the door. Choose it now. Let there be light.

*Now Meditate*

# INTENTION
## for the day

_____
_____
_____

☀ MORNING *writing*

_____
_____
_____
_____
_____
_____
_____
_____

☾ EVENING *reflections & gratitude*

_____
_____
_____
_____
_____
_____
_____

# 90.

# *I am* EMPOWERED
## BY MY SOUL'S URGE FOR
# *creative expression*

The power that gives rise to the universe is also the impulse behind artistic expression. It's sometimes called Divine Will, and it's yours to draw upon. The more you practice allowing your consciousness to expand beyond your body and mind (as in meditation), the more readily you can channel this infinite source of energy. It *wants* to be expressed through you, simply for the delight of expression.

The desire to create is the fundamental sacred urge from which all is born. When you tap into this plane of consciousness, your actions are bolstered by the Source. They reflect the prompting of your Inner Being. And they issue forth without strain or attachment.

If there's no opportunity for such expression in your work, it may eventually come to feel like it's draining the life out of you. But when the creative drive is given an outlet in your activities, you will be fed by them rather than taxed.

Today, offer yourself to the Divine Will. Open yourself to opportunities for creative expression, and feel how this wellspring empowers you.

*Now Meditate*

# INTENTION
## for the day

☀ MORNING *writing*

🌙 EVENING *reflections & gratitude*

# 91. *I* AM THE *light*

As you move through life, there is a light that goes with you everywhere. Have you noticed? When you look upon the world, it lets you see. In times of despair it seems barely a flashlight, but it must still be there if you are able to peer into the darkness, to perceive what seems broken or hopeless. How could you even recognize your shadow, your sadness, and your fear without a source of light? *Of course* there is a light. You *know* this. It has never departed and never will. It's so ever-present that perhaps you failed to notice it and didn't think to investigate its source.

It's you, silly.

*You* are the light.

People see it in your eyes. It shines through in your deeds. Even when you are immersed in pain and confusion, your basic nature – lightness – is unaffected. The perception of this light can be obscured by the veils of your humanity, but it can't be extinguished. Welcome it into your life and see your confusion burned away. As you embrace this identity, the light becomes you and gleams through you. It is your purpose. It guides your way and smiles upon the world.

*Now Meditate*

# INTENTION
## *for the day*

---

☀ MORNING *writing*

---

🌙 EVENING *reflections & gratitude*

# I HAVE PATIENCE
## FOR
## THOSE WHO ARE
## *asleep*
## AND
## *Confused*

The world is asleep in a dream of separation. Your fellow humans, by and large, believe they are separate from one another and their Source. They believe they are vulnerable, needy, alone, unsupported. They've tuned out their inner voice; they have blindfolded their inner vision; they have closed themselves off to Divine guidance. They have been hurt and they want to retaliate. They want connection, but they can't perceive that they're already connected. So they look for the next best things – approval, control, pleasure, security – and they bumble about, deaf and blind, managing to attain these things at whatever cost.

Have you ever seen cruelty among children on a playground? Excluding each other. Teasing the one who's different. Vying for each other's acceptance. Changing their allegiances from moment to moment. You don't condemn them because you understand that they're just trying to figure it out. But the same is true for most adults. They have bigger bodies but the same insecurities and confusion. They have bigger words and responsibilities, but the same consciousness resides in them, the same inner child trying to get what it needs.

Today, practice noticing this confusion in those who provoke you to relinquish your peace, and be patient and forgiving.

## ~ *Now Meditate* ~

# INTENTION
## for the day

_____

_____

☀ MORNING *writing*

_____

_____

_____

_____

_____

_____

_____

_____

☾ EVENING *reflections & gratitude*

_____

_____

_____

_____

_____

_____

_____

_____

# 93. I FORGIVE EVERYONE

## FOR EVERY *thought* AND *action*

## THAT HAS EVER *occurred*

If you want real freedom you need to be able to retire from the job of warden over the many prisoners from whom you withhold forgiveness, and this can only be done by pardoning everyone and everything.

In order for you to be completely free, there must be nothing left to forgive. Nothing and no one. Imagine how liberated you could feel if you had nothing against anyone or anything. No resentment, just total acceptance. Not just for the people and events in your own life, but for everything that has ever been thought or done in the whole history of the universe. This means recognizing the totality of the massive burden that weighs on our collective consciousness and shedding the *whole thing.*

Forgiveness is not the same as condoning brutality or treachery. If you forgive the rapists, murderers, and oppressors of the world this won't cause you to lose sight of what is and isn't aligned with Love. Nor will it invite more suffering. In fact, forgiveness is the only way to end the cycle of pain and separation that gives rise to such acts.

The deepest most complete forgiveness comes with the recognition that there was never any sin to begin with – not in the unforgivable sense. Only confusion. Only mistakes. There are so many confused children in the world. Some of them may be your parents, your teachers, your friends, your partner, you. True forgiveness enters this confusion with Light and Love. And the world will be forever changed.

## ∼ *Now Meditate* ∼

# INTENTION
## for the day

## ☀ MORNING *writing*

## ☾ EVENING *reflections & gratitude*

## 94. *As I claim my light, so is the world* ILLUMINATED

The world needs you. It awaits your light.

The world is you, an extension of your own being that only *seems* to be apart from you. There are dark corners that only you have access to. A billion wicks anticipate your flame.

## AWAKEN YOUR LUMINESCENCE

Claiming your light entails relinquishing all the small stories you've told about yourself. Let go of the perception of yourself as powerless and flawed. Release the belief that you can't make a difference, that you're *just one person*. Challenge the idea that embracing your power is arrogant, or that it will cause others to feel inferior.

Opening yourself to even a glimmer of your brilliance will make a difference. But awaken your luminescence in every particle of your being and the world will be forever changed.

*Now Meditate*

# INTENTION
## for the day

☀ MORNING *writing*

☾ EVENING *reflections & gratitude*

# 95. MY *purpose* TODAY
## IS TO
## LOVE THE WORLD
## *unconditionally*

Your love means more to the world, and more to *you*, than you know. Whatever you fill your day with, let your overarching purpose be to love the world without condition.

Remember, you're part of the world, so this means loving yourself, too. Because you are the portal through which this Love shines, don't let the blockage of self-love interfere with the outward expression of Love. And as you express Love to the outside world, this Love is simultaneously moving through you, so it's a gift to yourself. Moreover, as the world is all an extension of yourself, removing restrictions from the places you find difficult to love – loving them anyway – inevitably expands your freedom and contributes to the integration of your shadow aspect.

The breadth of this Love encompasses absolutely everything. Start with the people and objects you find easy to love. Let the Love build, let it warm you, melting your judgment, and then move into extending Love to the facets of your inner and outer world that are more difficult for you. Imagine your Love penetrating and enveloping these places, making them one with yourself. Finally, look into the darkest places, the deplorable aspects of the world and yourself, and fill them with your light.

Who would you be if you loved the world – every dimension of it – unconditionally?

## Now Meditate

# INTENTION
### for the day

_____
_____

## ☀ MORNING *writing*

_____
_____
_____
_____
_____
_____
_____
_____

## ☾ EVENING *reflections & gratitude*

_____
_____
_____
_____
_____
_____
_____

# 96. I CAN EXCHANGE MY

# burdens for grace

Offer your burden to God, ask that it be managed for you, and you will witness grace. There's just a little service fee: acceptance and commitment. Acceptance means you'll stop resisting it and commitment means you'll stick with your choice to let God manage it. If you truly give it to God, that means it's not yours to fix anymore. If you later discover you're resisting it again, you've taken it back. It's as if you've said, "Here, will you please take care of this? No, wait, let me deal with it. Ok, it's yours again. No, never mind, let me fight it for a while. . ."

Asking to exchange your burdens for grace isn't like taking a painkiller. You're not looking to remove the symptom while ignoring the deeper problem, you're asking to relinquish the whole problem.

Grace tends to come in one of two forms. The first is that the burden simply goes away. It disappears, gets resolved, or you experience a shift in perspective whereby you realize it wasn't actually a burden. The second is that you are shown the tools that will allow you to eliminate the burden. The latter scenario may not seem like as good of a deal, but we find it's what happens when you're "secretly" opposing the removal of the issue. In such cases, the mind believes the issue can't be overcome without going through some sort of process. Perhaps your soul asked for the opportunity to learn or experience something, to heal an old wound, to rectify an imbalance, to help someone, or to grow in a certain way. And this "burden" was orchestrated to serve that purpose.

When you're presented with such a challenge, there is no penalty for asking for God's help, nor any extra credit for figuring it out on your own. So, why not just ask for help – either from your human friends or the Divine – whenever you need it?

*Now Meditate*

# INTENTION
## for the day

---

☀ MORNING *writing*

---

☾ EVENING *reflections & gratitude*

# 97. There is nothing wrong

The crux of a grievance is wrongness. Your grievances shrink your consciousness and empower your ego, and at the heart of every one of them is the belief that something is *wrong*.

Besides causing you to generate grievances, the belief of wrongness perpetuates feelings of blame, entrapment, and instability. *This is not the way it should be,* you think. Wrongness is an ingredient in the thoughts that most distress you. And while it's possible for negative emotions to come and go in a healthy way, the *persistence* of an emotion such as sadness, fear, anger, grief, or worry indicates resistance and an underlying belief that something is wrong.

"Wrong" is an argument against reality. When you open your awareness beyond the wrong-seeing mind, it becomes harder to believe that anything is wrong. You can access this awareness in silent meditation or by actively bringing yourself back to the present. Ask yourself, "What is wrong in THIS VERY MOMENT?" And don't venture even a second into the past or the future. *Right now,* what is wrong? If you have any answer but, "Nothing," ask yourself how you know this to be true, and if you can know with absolute certainty that it's wrong.

Watch your thoughts for pronouncements of wrongness, and ask yourself, "What if there is nothing wrong?"

*Now Meditate*

# INTENTION
## for the day

☀ MORNING *writing*

☾ EVENING *reflections & gratitude*

# 98.

WHEN I *expand* MY CONSCIOUSNESS,

THE *world* IS *freed*

You may think that the way you hold the world in your mind affects only your own perception. But today we ask that you be open to another possibility – that the world outside you reflects the world inside you. Shift your perception – expand your consciousness, go beyond your everyday thinking, embrace your Highest Self, love and forgive the world – and then notice. How does the world respond?

## THE EXPANSION OF YOUR CONSCIOUSNESS IS INEVITABLE

In your mind, you argue with the world and seek to control it, you disdain parts of it and elevate others. It's not truly enslaved, but it acts that way, full as it is of people who live within the strict confines they co-construct.

But the expansion of your consciousness is inevitable, as the natural resolution of a lifetime of *concealment* of your true Divinity. With this expansion, the world will be freed.

*Now Meditate*

# INTENTION
## for the day

※ MORNING *writing*

☾ EVENING *reflections & gratitude*

# 99.
## Contraction DOESN'T MEAN I'm on the wrong path

Expansion and contraction are the way of the Universe. Tides ebb and flow. Breath goes in and out. Life opens and closes. Truth is concealed and revealed. Thus, most experiences of expansion are followed by some degree of contraction.

When you expand, you outgrow your image of yourself, which can feel uncomfortable or unsafe. And the more you consciously transcend your ego, the more threatened your ego feels. So it devises ways to pull you back in – to contract you back to its narrow confines. It accomplishes this primarily by generating conflict and discomfort. If you "take the bait" and engage in the conflict or resist the discomfort, you empower your ego and ensure that it remains indispensable.

Your response to contraction determines how hard it hits you. If it causes you to dive back into old personality structures, return to bad habits, attack the world, or believe you're having a massive setback, you're likely to contract more and for longer. But if you refuse to take the bait – if you see it for what it is – you'll move through it more swiftly and easily.

Learn to recognize contraction. Know that it's part of a natural cycle. You're on the right path. Breathe through the urge to resist. See if you can expand your consciousness enough to see this pattern from the "outside." Is there an opportunity to let go of something that will facilitate a greater re-expansion?

Tell yourself, "I am in sync with the breath of the Universe."

## ∽ Now Meditate ∽

# INTENTION
*for the day*

## ☀ MORNING *writing*

## ☾ EVENING *reflections & gratitude*

# 100.

# *Every*

## CONTRACTION

## *preludes a greater*

# EXPANSION

While it's important to recognize the role that egoic self-preservation plays in contraction, in actuality contraction is more than this. Seen in the big picture, contraction isn't pathological but a necessary phase in awakening and an essential counterpart to expansion.

Every facet of your belief system and self-image will eventually need to give way in order to for you to expand into your Highest Self. Imagine a semi-inflated balloon with several small rubber bands wrapped around it. As you blow up the balloon, each of these bands will at some point restrict the further expansion of the balloon and require removal. You may need to let some of the air out of the balloon in order to slip the band off without damaging the balloon.

In a similar way, as you expand, you'll find at a certain point that you're restrained by, say, the belief that life is hard, or the identity of "I am a nurse." You may then experience a contraction so that you can *meet this restriction* and slip it off. In doing so, you're now able to expand beyond what you thought was possible . . . until you meet the restriction of the next rubber band.

Your contractions indicate that you've outgrown your previous limitations. Every contraction is an opportunity to see how you've grown. In this process you will be served by trusting, feeling willingly, breathing deeply, staying open and curious, and forgiving.

## ∽ *Now Meditate* ∽

# INTENTION
*for the day*

## ☀ MORNING *writing*

## ☾ EVENING *reflections & gratitude*

# 101.

# I *Trust*

## IN THE WAYS OF THE UNIVERSE

Trust may not arise naturally if it's left up to your mind. It sees an unpredictable world that seems to guarantee pain and hardship. It tends to think, "I'll trust when I see a world in which there's no risk of suffering." But as long as humans have free will, suffering will remain an option.

So, ask your mind, what does *not* trusting do for you? Does it make you more prepared for tragedy? Does it make you better able to handle hardship? Does it make you happy? Or does it consume energy and make you ill at ease?

And what might be possible if you were to trust?

The first thing you'll experience is *ease;* you can *rest* in trust. Even if you don't understand how the Universe works, if you trust, there's no need to resist or control it. You can allow life to unfold on its own. Next, you'll begin to reclaim the energy you've been exerting toward shielding yourself against all the bad things that might happen. And finally, you'll begin to see magic everywhere. Serendipities, gifts, and grace.

If the word "Universe" here feels too impersonal, feel free to put your trust in your own Highest Self, in Love, in God, in your Divine Mother, or whatever expression of the Oneness is easiest for you to connect with. Then practice surrendering to it.

What do you have to lose? If you want to experience trust and it isn't coming naturally, try this: trust *anyway* and see what happens. Will you be guaranteed a life without hardship? No, but if you sincerely trust, you'll be guided through it, you will see more blessings than hardship, and you'll come to *know* that you will be okay no matter what.

## ~ *Now Meditate* ~

# INTENTION
*for the day*

## ☀ MORNING *writing*

## ☾ EVENING *reflections & gratitude*

# 102.

## I choose my Highest Self

Who has *authority* over your experience? The identity you created or your True Self? Is your limited, power hungry mind dominating the show? Or are you guided by the vast, fearless Consciousness that you really are? You are presented with this choice in every moment, and like all humans, you probably give authority to your mind the great majority of the time.

When you begin to choose Spirit – over and over, with ever greater conviction – your everyday awareness will start to expand. Your thoughts and emotions will be less apt to run away with you. You'll see your mind's attention-grabbing tactics with greater clarity. And the inklings of awakening will visit you more frequently.

Practice these statements today – and forever:

> *I choose Spirit.*
>
> *I choose my Highest Self.*
>
> *I withdraw my attention from my ego and offer it to Divine Light.*
>
> *I give authority over my being to my Highest Self.*

Notice what happens when you say these statements or your own variations on them. Be prepared for your desperate mind to lull you with distraction and engage your emotions in conflict and drama. And *remember* the true peace and unfathomable joy that are your birthright.

### Now Meditate

# INTENTION
*for the day*

## ☀ MORNING *writing*

## ☾ EVENING *reflections & gratitude*

# 103.
## EVERY *moment* HOLDS AN *opportunity* FOR ME TO *expand*

We previously used the word *expansion* to indicate the growth or awakening of *you* into *YOU*. That is, the expansion of your human self into your Source. In this lesson we aim to convey the mutuality of this process. That is, expansion is also the process whereby Source gets to venture into new territory *through you*. You are the frontier of the expansion of Source and Source is the frontier of your expansion.

Source expands through you regardless of your conscious participation in the process, but every moment holds an opportunity to *facilitate* this process, which is a satisfying experience. You can do this by asking your Inner Self how it wants to expand. In your meditation, you might request, "Show me how you would like us to expand together."

Here are some of our own suggestions for facilitating expansion. Consciously enter the experience at hand. What happens when you move into that task, when you *become* the task? Broaden the layers of yourself that you're able to identify with. Experience yourself beyond your body, mind, feelings, and possessions. Unite with more of the world. See others' perspectives, share lovingkindness, look past the differences. And say *yes* to what's happening.

Whatever task you're engaged in, whomever you're speaking with, there is always an opportunity for you to expand. As you allow your consciousness to encompass whatever is at hand, saying, "Yes" to all of it, your sense of Self grows. As you say to everything you encounter, "I Am This," the effect is not one of acquisition or feeding the ego, but of becoming more than any of these things, more of what you really are. This expansion of perspective dwarfs the ego. You can *be* with more and more of reality in a state of peace and acceptance.

Let go of whatever is contracting you. Open to whatever is in front of you. Become the Universe.

*Now Meditate*

# INTENTION
## for the day

☀ MORNING *writing*

🌙 EVENING *reflections & gratitude*

## 104.

# *Everything* I SEE

## IS THE PLAY OF

# *Divine Love*

Divine Love, which is what you are and all that is, is constantly expressing itself in infinite ways through the process of Divine Play. The word "play" is meant to convey that this expression is done *for its own sake – for the love of it –* rather than for some end result. Rather than winding up to some grand plan at a later date, the fullness of this Love is already here now and always.

God in its unmanifest state emerges as form so that it can experience itself – and love itself – in all possible ways. It holds this form for a period and then retracts from the form, to be reabsorbed back into its unmanifest Self, only to emerge again in another form.

Does viewing the world this way change how you relate to your life?

Everything you see is the play of Divine Love.

## *Now Meditate*

# INTENTION
### for the day

## ☀ MORNING *writing*

## ☾ EVENING *reflections & gratitude*

# 105. *Today* I AM *Enlightened*

It may not feel like you're enlightened. You don't seem to be perpetually aware of your oneness with everything, and perhaps you're still at the mercy of your thoughts and emotions. But what if you *are* enlightened, and this is all part of a silly, elaborate dream? A dream you'll wake up from with *such* relief, because you'll *remember* that there's nothing to fear, that all is Love, and that you are free. For now, though, since that reality is so clearly preferable to this dream, why not embody that way of being?

Ask yourself throughout the day, "Who would I be and how would I act in this moment if I were *awake?*" How do you respond differently to something that would usually annoy you? How do you experience mundane tasks differently from this perspective? What is possible in your interactions with other humans? With beauty? With ugliness?

In all experiences you perceive connection. You see opportunities for greater awakening or to awaken others. You recognize the impact of your ways. You feel your power and you know how to use it for the highest good for everyone involved. You are light. You are imperturbable.

At the end of the day, ask yourself, "How was this an enhancement to my day?" Even if these behaviors and perspectives don't arise automatically in you, consider that you were able to *choose* them anyway. Why not continue to do so?

*Liberation … means going from the experience of being trapped in your life situation to the experience of continuously perceiving that you are the infinite creative Light of divine Presence, joyously playing the role of a wife, or mother, or doctor, and doing so in service to all beings.*

- Christopher Wallis in *Tantra Illuminated*

*Now Meditate*

# INTENTION
## for the day

☀ MORNING *writing*

☾ EVENING *reflections & gratitude*

# 106.
## *The Divine works through me to* FIND MYSELF *in everything*

As a baby, you went through a most gratifying process of discovering, part by part, that this body is *you*. One day your limbs flailed wildly, and the next they were an extension of your consciousness.

## I AM THIS

Now you get to experience that same process of discovery with the world beyond your body. You may not have conscious control over these parts, but you will nonetheless experience a *recognition* in all of them. A recognition of Self. This. Is. Me.

When you behold something – a blade of grass, perhaps, or a cell phone – try to be completely present with it. Give it the entire bandwidth of your attention. See God in it. And say, "I am this."

## *Now Meditate*

# INTENTION
## for the day

☀ MORNING *writing*

☾ EVENING *reflections & gratitude*

# 107.
# I
# *awaken*
## TO MY
# *true identity*

You've been in a sort of sleep. Dreaming a dream in which you often feel confused about the rules of the game, in which death is inevitable, evil is rampant, and conflict is everywhere. There are good parts, too, but they never last forever. The truth is, your life is much more than this. Perhaps it's time to wake up.

The dream state is essentially a consequence of focusing your attention on only a very narrow band of reality – primarily your mind and feelings, and also your body and possessions – and believing this to be all that you are.

But these blinders have kept you from seeing all the colors, hearing all the sounds, and most importantly, feeling the unfathomable Love and understanding what you really are.

Rather than seeing God as an all-powerful being who created the world at arm's length, as something separate from itself to watch over and be entertained by, like a civilization-building video game, consider a different scenario – where God emerges *as* the world, equally present in all things. And you are that.

*Now Meditate*

# INTENTION
## for the day

☀ MORNING *writing*

☾ EVENING *reflections & gratitude*

# 108. I am the One who is experiencing itself as all of creation

What if you could experience yourself as the human life you embody without losing your awareness of the Supreme Oneness that you are, which contains and sustains that life? As long as you reside in this body, your human mini-consciousness may never be able to fully grasp the vastness that you are, but it's well within your ability to experience it.

Imagine if you were a leaf who knows nothing of trees. You emerge in the spring as a bright, tiny bud; you unfurl, shiny and green; you bask in the sun, transforming light into nourishment; you change to reds and yellows; and you eventually dry out and flutter to the earth, all along believing you're a lone leaf among a world of leaves, oblivious to this *tree* that sustains you and unites you with all the other leaves. Today, experience yourself as the tree.

As an alternative to your usual mode of being completely immersed in playing the part of the person whose body you inhabit, practice choosing to consciously embody more of the unbounded Awareness that you are. Remind yourself, "I am God experiencing life through this human."

*Now Meditate*

# INTENTION
## for the day

☀ MORNING *writing*

☾ EVENING *reflections & gratitude*

# CONCLUSION

Thank you for joining us on this soul adventure. Thank you for your willingness to do the work, to meet your shadow, and to be uncomfortable. Thank you for the bravery to open yourself to new possibilities. Thank you for your devotion to healing, and for recognizing your role in the healing and awakening of the world.

As we see it, this process is an act of love for yourself, initiated by your Divine Consciousness, which loves you with a completeness that's almost unfathomable to the mind. This book is just one of the many communications sprinkled throughout the world by your Highest Self to remind you of your True Nature.

It has been said that one of the hurdles to the mind's ability to grasp Reality is its inability to reconcile *paradoxes*. Keep this in mind as you continue with your work. You may discover that even while you experience the world as perfect just as it is, you nonetheless notice yourself drawn to facilitate change. The world doesn't need to be seen as wrong in order for us to find opportunities for greater awakeness, freer freedom, and lighter light. In the words of Jesuit priest and author, Anthony de Mello, "Everything is a mess and all is well."

It has also been said that the truth is simple – if it were complicated, everyone would get it. Remember this, too, as you return to your complicated life. We can't all be ascetics living in caves; that's the easy path. Instead, we "householders" have the tricky task of navigating relationships, possessions, politics, careers, and money without getting manipulated by it and succumbing to complication. This is all the more challenging in the Information Age when there's a torrent of data rushing through our minds. But there's a silver lining to the burden of complication.

In simpler times, change came slowly and it was uncommon to make a dramatic alteration to the course of one's life. But in these complex times, there's an exponential acceleration of change. The world can be intensely polarized and life sometimes feels like a rollercoaster. However, it also means that awakening is available to anyone and everyone – regardless of karma, socio-economic background, or how much counseling you've had. In fact, the best time for transformation is often in the midst of chaos. When a person is determined to see the simplicity – the Unity – through the craziness, everything can turn around. Remember, the truth is simple.

When we *all* decide that waking up to our Unity is worth prioritizing, the world will change dramatically. Perhaps the next evolution of the human species will be initiated through a mass shift of consciousness rather than favorable genes. We envision a world where people live in the freedom of being able to experience the Divine in everything – and themselves as the Divine.

We hope this process has inspired you to devote yourself to this work in an ongoing way. Keep checking in each morning. Choose consciously what to feed your mind as you're waking up. Meditate! Set an intention for the day. Throughout the day, bring your consciousness into your body, breathing down into your pelvic bowl and letting go of whatever comes up. In the evening, keep up your practice of releasing the day and expressing your gratitude.

Consider going through the book again. Every time you do it, you'll understand it at a deeper level, in a different way, and perhaps with greater receptivity. Or do another process if you like. Just stay engaged with *something* that reminds you that you are the Supreme Consciousness experiencing life as a human.

There's no limit to what you can get out of this work. The journey doesn't end here. If you're interested in going further with us, check out our *What's Next* page at www.ritualsfortransformation.com/whatsnext

We have the deepest gratitude and utmost respect for you.

*Thank you.*

Love,

*Briana & Peter*

Briana & Dr. Peter Borten

When we *all* decide that waking up to our Unity is worth prioritizing, the world will change dramatically. Perhaps the next evolution of the human species will be initiated through a mass shift of consciousness rather than favorable genes. We envision a world where people live in the freedom of being able to experience the Divine in everything – and themselves as the Divine.

We hope this process has inspired you to devote yourself to this work in an ongoing way. Keep checking in each morning. Choose consciously what to feed your mind as you're waking up. Meditate! Set an intention for the day. Throughout the day, bring your consciousness into your body, breathing down into your pelvic bowl and letting go of whatever comes up. In the evening, keep up your practice of releasing the day and expressing your gratitude.

Consider going through the book again. Every time you do it, you'll understand it at a deeper level, in a different way, and perhaps with greater receptivity. Or do another process if you like. Just stay engaged with *something* that reminds you that you are the Supreme Consciousness experiencing life as a human.

There's no limit to what you can get out of this work. The journey doesn't end here. If you're interested in going further with us, check out our *What's Next* page at www.ritualsfortransformation.com/whatsnext

We have the deepest gratitude and utmost respect for you.

*Thank you.*

Love,

Briana & Dr. Peter Borten